PRE-SCHOOL EDUCATION TODAY

This book is published under the auspices of the Council for Public Schools, Inc., of 16 Arlington Street, Boston, Massachusetts. The Council is a national group of laymen and scholars established in 1962 to sponsor the development and production of new courses of study for the public schools.

PRE-SCHOOL EDUCATION TODAY

NEW APPROACHES TO TEACHING
THREE-, FOUR-, AND FIVE-YEAR-OLDS

Edited by Fred M. Hechinger

Doubleday & Company, Inc., Garden City, New York
1966

"Early Social Environment: Its Influence on School Adaptation," by Martin Deutsch. Reprinted from *The School Dropout*, ed. D. Schreiber. Washington, D.C.: National Education Association, 1964.

"The Psychological Basis for Using Pre-School Enrichment as an Antidote for Cultural Deprivation," by J. McVicker Hunt. Appeared in the *Merrill-Palmer Quarterly of Behavior and Development,* Vol. 10, No. 3, July 1964.

"Facilitating Development in the Pre-School Child: Social and Psychological Perspectives," by Martin Deutsch. Appeared in the *Merrill-Palmer Quarterly of Behavior and Development,* Vol. 10, No. 3, July 1964.

"A Pre-School Enrichment Program for Disadvantaged Children," by Shirley Feldmann. Reprinted from *The New Era,* 45:3, 1964.

"An Academically Oriented Pre-School for Culturally Deprived Children," by Carl Bereiter, Siegfried Engelman, Jean Osborn, and Philip A. Reidford. From a symposium on "Acceleration of Intellectual Development in Early Childhood" at the American Educational Research Convention, February 12, 1965. Not published elsewhere.

"A Saturday School for Mothers and Pre-Schoolers," by Margaret Lipchik. Reprinted from *The National Elementary Principal,* Vol. XLIV, No. 2, November 1964.

Bibliography appearing in the IRCD Bulletin, March 1965, a publication of the Information Retrieval Center on the Disadvantaged, Ferkauf Graduate School of Education, Yeshiva University, New York.

Contents

Preface

The idea for this book originated with Graham T. Winslow, Chairman of the Council for Public Schools, Inc., who realized that the widespread enthusiasm for new departures in pre-school education should not proceed without some readily available background information. It was because of his concern for, and familiarity with, the workings of public education that he recognized the risks facing new programs that start with an abundance of gusto and even funds but with a dearth of experience. Thus, the project of this basic primer was conceived.

When I asked the advice of John W. Gardner, then President of the Carnegie Corporation of New York, he agreed that a rapidly produced small volume of basic readings would be of great service to the development of pre-school education, and the work of compilation and selection was begun.

After completion of the basic selection, John H. Fischer, President of Teachers College, Columbia University, and Francis Chase, then Dean of the Graduate School of Education of the University of Chicago, devoted much of their valuable time in reviewing the selected material. Their suggestions for changes and additions were invaluable; their general approval of both the enterprise and the specific presentation of research and background material gave vital aid and comfort to the editor. My thanks go to them and all others who have helped in this enterprise.

F. M. H.

PRE-SCHOOL EDUCATION TODAY

So, then, to every man his chance—to every man regardless of his birth, his shining, golden opportunity—
to every man the right to live, to work, to be himself,
and to become whatever thing his manhood and his
vision can combine to make him—this, seeker, is the
promise of America.

THOMAS WOLFE
You Can't Go Home Again

1. Passport to Equality

Fred M. Hechinger[1]

Pre-school education has become a fact; the danger now is
that it may become a fad.

The idea of pre-school education is not by any means new
and revolutionary. Almost every society in which parents
needed to be away from home has devised some form of pre-
school care and training. In Scandinavia, for example, it has
long been routine in many factories to provide daytime child
care centers, even for infants, to permit working mothers to
"check in" their children as they report to work.

It is hardly surprising therefore that America, challenged
to provide truly equal opportunities for millions of children
from desperately poor and underprivileged homes, is turning
to pre-school education as a way out of a terrible dilemma.
The nature of the dilemma is easily stated. Amid unprece-
dented prosperity and in plain view of the most conspicuous

[1] Fred M. Hechinger is Education Editor of *The New York Times*.

consumption imaginable, there remain pockets of abject poverty. Most, though not all, of the children who grow up in this environment of poverty amid plenty also belong to the ethnic minorities—mainly Negro and Puerto Rican—who find the color line a cruel barrier.

Although the law has made it an illegal barrier, fully to overcome the psychological obstacles of color within a predominantly white society will take time. Meanwhile there is no question whatever that the road to equal opportunity for the racial minorities must be paved by education.

And there's the rub. To expect that Negro children need only be admitted to school on a basis of equality with white children to be assured full participation in the affluent society is sentimental and over-optimistic, a naïve pipedream. In fact, it is exactly because success in formal schooling has become so vital to success in contemporary America that inability to compete for such success has been turned into a seemingly insuperable handicap.

All the evidence today indicates that children from a home background that not only is economically and socially at the lowest level but lacks family orientation toward formal learning are virtually excluded from success in school. They are preconditioned for failure. The school, attuned as it is to the middle-class majority, seldom helps such children catch up; it often actually (though unwittingly) widens the gap between success and failure.

Skill with words and comprehension of ideas that sprout from the thoughts behind words are probably the most essential prerequisites for formal learning. Yet, these are exactly the skills most lacking in the slum child. The contrast between him and his middle-class contemporary is painfully sharp. The middle-class home is child-oriented, often to a fault. Parents dote on their infants' first words. This concern for early skill with the language—the bright, funny, precocious sayings—grows until it probably reaches its zenith around the ages of four and five, when mothers and fathers can still take most of the credit for such early development. If the home is well stocked with reading matter, the drive toward verbal success is even more intense.

By the same token, the middle-class parent welcomes and encourages questions, explorations and—within reasonable limits—even a certain amount of damage done by an adventuresome child. Mothers are virtually obsessed with ways of exploiting—even pushing—the natural curiosity of infants; see the mass sales of books about infant behavior and about the best ways of answering or extracting young children's questions.

By contrast, the slum home is a place of little opportunity for infants to talk, question, and seek answers. In an overcrowded tenement, curiosity is a nuisance. In daytime, the most competent adults are out trying to make a living, and the children are either left to their older brothers and sisters or are parked with the least competent woman in the building or on the block—the one who is unable to find a job. When the parents return, after the frustration of a day in the slum dweller's life, the atmosphere hardly encourages much concern with child care à la Dr. Spock. There is little patience with childish talk and questions. The passive child is considered the good child.

J. W. Getzels, Professor of Education at the University of Chicago, put the problem into statistical perspective in his working paper on pre-school education, prepared for the 1965 White House Conference on Education. He pointed out, first, that the issue is not a new one. More than a generation ago, R. S. and H. M. Lynd showed in their classic study of "Middletown" that by the time a child entered school, he was already typed intellectually by his parents' economic status. Although only 13.4 per cent of Business Class children in the first grade were below 90 in IQ, fully 42.5 per cent of the Working Class children were below that level. The Lynds put the question, which is now being raised again so urgently, in these technical words: To what extent was this observed difference in intelligence a reflection of the "modification of native endowment by varying environmental conditions?" It is the question which today is being explored in greater detail and with far more current sociological and pragmatic urgency by such experts as Benjamin S. Bloom in his experimental work and his recent book, *Stability and Change in Human Characteristics,* and in clinical-pedagogical application by Dr. Bruno Bettelheim.

Dr. Getzels, in his paper, cited Dr. Bloom's findings and his estimate that the long-term over-all effect of living in a culturally deprived as against a culturally abundant environment is likely to be 20 IQ points—an enormous difference in terms of society's and the school's expectations. It may well signify the difference between a youngster who is thought to be barely educable for unskilled labor and one who is college "material." Yet—and this is the point made by Dr. Bloom—the change in environment may transform the same child from low to high potential.

The Bloom hypothesis, cited by Dr. Getzels, is that the 20-point IQ difference is, in terms of a slum child's development, spaced as follows: from birth to four years of age, 10 IQ units; from four to eight years of age, 6 IQ units; from eight to seventeen, 4 IQ units.

The implications are obvious. The most serious harm, in terms of real or potential retardation, is already done by the time the slum child reaches what for the privileged child is the nursery school age. When the slum child enters school, he has been permitted to drop behind so drastically—almost to the full extent of his eventual and possibly permanent limitation—that school means competition for what, in many instances, must be unattainable success. The stage is set, not for learning but for frustration. Add to it the impact of both the white folklore about the inferiority of the non-white and the impact, too, of the Negro child's damaging self-image, and school can easily turn into a breeding place of white prejudice and black despair.

Faced by this dilemma, one group of liberal educational and sociological observers proposes that the remedy must be found in an abandoning of the school's middle-class goals and standards. Those who advocate this remedy say that the lower class child has cultural standards and strengths of his own. Since survival in the slums unquestionably requires a kind of ingenuity and toughness, which the pampered middle-class child lacks, this thesis is easy to document.

The fallacy of the argument, however, is the assumption that minorities can "make it" to success without adjusting to the goals and standards of the majority. This does not rule out the usefulness of certain traits derived from the lower class environment or the possibility of utilizing those traits in the classroom. This introduction of such traits, after all, is what has generally been sought in any quest for "new blood"— in business, government, families and civilizations. Such infusions have made the newcomers a source of strength and vitality. This is sometimes resented by the established order, but in general it is accepted—even to the point of feeding the favored mythology of the self-made man, the rough diamond and the poor boy who, in best women's magazine fiction style, marries the wealthy girl and takes over Dad's respected but declining business.

Romanticized as these stories are, they are based on accepted social philosophy. They allow no basis for the well-intentioned, sentimental demands that the "culturally deprived" child is not deprived at all but merely hears a drummer from another culture. Even if this were true, the road to success would most likely still remain the road to successful operation within the majority culture. It is surely misguided to think of the slums—or of the brutally imposed life of exclusion suffered as the result of the white supremacy myth—as just another culture to be accepted and made permanent. Such a view results from idyllic confusion of cultural deprivation with the romanticism of The Noble Savage. Despite its flawless intentions, it is merely systematized failure and frustration. In the end, it invites open warfare: it sets the two worlds —white affluence and black ghetto—permanently apart as hostile camps, frozen into different societal worlds.

Recognition of the facts of deprivation and of the needs of slum children or their equivalent in rural distressed areas has logically led to the pre-school movement. The argument in favor of such education is virtually unanswerable: if deprivation starts to build up at an early age and progressively limits and eventually blocks entry into the mainstream of society, then an early start must be made to offset the lack of parental teaching, care and mind-molding.

This is, in basic terms, the idea of pre-school education for deprived children. On it has been based most of today's experimentation. On it, too, are pinned high hopes of educators and politicians who want to end the frustration of the deprived and to lead children from exclusion to full participation in the responsibilities and rewards of modern society.

This is why, for the first time, substantial amounts of money have become available for the pre-school experiment. Such money is included in the new Federal school aid bills; it is offered even more liberally in the so-called War Against Poverty of the Office of Economic Opportunity; it is increasingly part of foundation- and government-sponsored research; it was a crucial part of the Great Cities grants made by the Ford Foundation in an effort to halt the decline of the often de facto segregated "inner cities" of the great urban centers.

Sparked by such interest and financial support, it is inevitable that business—the educational technology, textbook publishers, manufacturers of toys and classroom or playground equipment—will enter the new pre-school field with enthusiasm and often with an eye toward quick profits.

School administrators, teachers, school board members and political leaders thus will be required to make intelligent choices and decisions—often based on nothing more than noble hopes and semi-informed hearsay. This is why this basic primer has been put together.

It is not intended to be a definitive selection. Before such a volume can be attempted years of experience may be necessary. What is needed now is an honest reader, containing a selection of some of the most basic papers of philosophy, experimentation, research, and observation.

The total amount of useful, written documentation currently available is small; within that total, the number of papers sufficiently readable to aid the teacher, principal, superintendent, school board member, city council official, or member of a legislature is even smaller. Some good papers had to be omitted—merely because they would add little to what had already been said in others. Some reports and research documents were eliminated because to publish them prematurely for wide, popular consumption would be a disservice to their authors.

It would furthermore be a disservice to suggest that any of the examples cited in subsequent chapters are typical of *all* pre-school efforts or should be regarded as such. Dr. Getzels, in his instructions to the White House Conference delegates, ably stressed this point. "The number and diversity of compensatory pre-school projects are growing so rapidly that it is hazardous to say anything about *the* nature of the programs without risk of oversimplifying and being out of date at once," he wrote.

Dr. Getzels' example of diversity, even within a small area, is worth keeping in mind. He said:

"Within walking distance of the University of Chicago are several separate programs. One is in a long-established predominantly middle-class nursery. The proposed curriculum includes free play, group games, show and tell, and neighbor-

hood trips—activities which do not differ from what is done
regularly in this nursery. Another is in the local public school,
which has never dealt with nursery or pre-kindergarten children—middle or lower class. Among the stated aims are to
give the children experience with the tools of learning—pencils,
crayons, books, etc.—and to develop their readiness for regular school activities. A third program which grew out of a volunteer college student project was designed specifically for
culturally deprived children. The staff was selected on the
basis of experience in pre-school education with such children, and there is heavy emphasis on auditory and visual discrimination, rhythmics, and self-expression. A fourth program
is in a local Montessori School, and will presumably be influenced by its philosophy and methods. From among the
Montessori activities are included 'practical life' projects (e.g.,
buttoning, tying, cleaning dishes, polishing copper, peeling
carrots) and there is emphasis on the ability to 'look at, see
and handle materials.' "

Dr. Getzels underlined the diversity by pointing to a recent
inventory of pre-school programs (not including Head Start,
the short-term summer program), undertaken by Dr. Robert
D. Hess at the University of Chicago. It showed that pre-
school programs were in operation in close to seventy cities.
Over half of these have been established within the past two
years. Their personnel, Dr. Hess reported, ranged from two
teachers, a social worker, two psychologists, and a nurse for
32 children to six teachers and thirty-six teacher-aides for
240 children.

To make the analysis of this diversity less perplexing, Dr.
Getzels suggests classifying all of them in three broad categories: the first assumes that the observed deficiencies of the
deprived children are more superficial than fundamental—the
differences are in quantity rather than in kind—and the pre-
school experiences that are needed are supplementary; the
second assumes that the significant deficiencies are in the lack

of familiarity with school-related objects and activities—say, pencils, books, the use of crayons, following directions—and the pre-school experiences must be predominantly academic-preparatory; the third assumes that because of powerful environmental effects the deprived child becomes fundamentally different in language and values, and the pre-school program thus becomes highly specialized in efforts to compensate for or counteract the environment.

The readings in this primer, however, must be prefaced by a warning. It is exactly because the social crisis and the potential of pre-school education are both so real—the one pressing and the other promising—that the danger of turning a new trend into a fad must be recognized and averted.

The search for solutions—a way out of the slums and an answer to the just demands of the civil rights leadership—is frantic. On the success of any action now taken depends a great deal, not least of all social peace in a society which, at least in the crowded urban centers, is on the brink of disastrous warfare. The pre-school experiment sounds so logical and so promising that it has begun to appear to some of those embroiled in the political and educational battle as a magic escape hatch.

Unfortunately, the history of education is paved with good intentions that have led to failure. Those who know the limitations of people as well as of educational methods are well aware that no miracle can assure easy success.

Yet, there are danger signs that the pre-school venture will, by some naïve or opportunistic persons, be treated as patent medicine—oversold as a sure cure, followed by the fatal letdown of disappointment.

Serious warnings have been sounded by the most successful and dedicated pioneer of the movement, Dr. Martin Deutsch, Director of the Institute for Developmental Studies of the New York Medical College's Department of Psychiatry.

"There is more interest in pre-school programs than is

supported by the knowledge we now have," Dr. Deutsch said. "There seems to be a feeling that putting a good deal of money into special education programs will stop violence in the streets. . . . I just don't think this is the case."

Dr. Deutsch stated: "There is tremendous pressure to set up programs without adequate preparation and training of teachers and without a well-developed curriculum. I think that greater immediate emphasis should be placed on universal kindergarten, with reduced pupil-teacher ratio." (It should be remembered, in the midst of the great enthusiasm for pre-school programs, that there are no kindergartens for about half of the nation's 4.1 million five-year-olds.)

Such concern was reflected also in the discussion of the pre-school concept at the White House Conference on Education. Virtually all experimenters agreed that, in order to succeed, a number of important cautions must be kept in mind.

(1) Dealing with the deprived three- or four-year-old child is not just a baby-sitting operation. Nor is it something that can automatically be expected from routinely trained kindergarten teachers. A great deal must first be known about the nature of the slum household. The search is for a program with a delicate balance between order and freedom—the order of steady routine lacking in the slum home and the freedom to explore, ask questions, and expect answers from adults, so important a part of middle-class child-rearing.

(2) Giving the deprived child a quick, one-shot pre-school opportunity simply is not enough. There is already highly disturbing evidence that the advantages gained from such a program, while beneficial as the child enters first grade, are quickly lost. Unless the process is continuing and the successful methods of induction into the majority culture are carried into the regular school process as well, the early gain quickly turns into illusion and possibly even greater frustrations. Some of the experimenters talk about the pre-school efforts as a sort of immunization. This is a useful parallel, but only if it

is remembered that immunization, without the proper boosters, wears off and fails to protect.

"What I would hope for," said Dr. Deutsch, "is a move toward an early childhood concept, running from three years of age to the end of third grade, with early childhood centers built into the architectural plans of the schools."

Thus, instead of being a flashy one-shot affair, pre-school education will have to be built into the school curriculum.

(3) Despite the impressive amounts of money which now appear to be available for pre-school education, the dollar signs are deceptive. The available funds are impressive only in terms of pilot projects; if the programs are to be translated into mass-ventures, the danger remains one of under- rather than over-financing. The surest way to defeat the new movement would be to spread the funds too thin. To create the impression that such efforts as Dr. Deutsch's, carried out as they are with a wealth of highly trained people, can be applied in cut-rate fashion to hundreds of thousands of children is to foster an illusion and invite cruel disillusionment.

Dr. Deutsch has estimated that between $1000 and $1200 per child a year is necessary for a good pre-school program, whereas at present allocations of between $400 and $500 are typical.

(4) It is vitally important that adults in the slums—preferably parents—become involved in the pre-school programs. This means that those in charge of the programs must reach out to the homes and, wherever possible, start to transform the children's home environment, too. At least they must make that environment friendly toward, and understanding of, the schools' efforts and goals.

None of these cautions should dampen enthusiasm for the pre-school approach. The pitfalls, though they must be avoided, have not been cited here as excuses to abandon the still unknown terrain. On the contrary, the explorations can and should be intensified, sometimes even over the protests and excessive doubts of the experimenters themselves whose pace is better attuned to the laboratory than to the desperate needs of the street. The only reason for these warnings is to avert failure by preventing the non-experts, no matter how pure their intentions, from watering down the experts' powerful prescription or from expecting instant miracles.

One last word. The time for the pre-school experiment is doubly right. That it is needed for the sake of the excluded and deprived is self-evident; but the movement is gathering momentum at the very moment when educational psychologists are offering persuasive evidence that all children can learn—and often want to learn—much more, much sooner. What has been introduced as a lifesaving device for those at the bottom of our society's ladder may, in time, help to loosen the rigidity of the educational structure as a whole.

2. Early Social Environment: Its Influence on School Adaptation

Martin Deutsch[1]

THE CHILD'S PREPARATION FOR SCHOOL

Generally speaking, the middle-class child is more likely than others to have the importance of school imprinted in his consciousness from the earliest possible age. This is not necessarily bad or good for the child or the school, but it is very different from the preparation of the lower social status child. I have never seen a school curriculum that is organized on the basis of the existence of these differences. Though these differences are sometimes acknowledged, both sets of children nevertheless are asked to climb the same mountain at the same rate, as if they had similar prior experience and training.

The lower class child, because of poorer preparation, is at a real disadvantage in this mountain climbing, though it is the middle-class child who probably has more personal anxiety about the success of his climb. However, the middle-class child has available to him other avenues for handling the school situation. There is more likely to be contiguity of the school-faculty orientation with his home-family orientation. Failure can be interpreted to him in appropriate and familiar terms, and methods of coping with it can be incorporated— increasing the motivation or offering the necessary rewards, goals, or punishments to effect the desired change in per-

[1] Martin Deutsch is Director of the Institute for Developmental Studies and Professor of Psychiatry at the New York Medical College. This article appeared in *The School Dropout*, ed. D. Schreiber (Washington, D.C.: National Education Association, 1964).

formance. For the middle-class child, the school is very central and is continuous with the totality of his life experiences. As a result, there are few incongruities between his school experiences and any others he is likely to have had, and there are intrinsic motivating and molding properties in the school situation to which he has been highly sensitized.

For the lower class child there is not the same contiguity or continuity, and he does not have the same coping mechanisms for internalizing success or psychologically surviving failure in the formal learning setting. If the lower class child starts to fail, he does not have the same kinds of operationally significant and functionally relevant support from his family or community—or from the school—that his counterpart has. Furthermore, because of the differences in preparation, he is more likely to experience failure. It might even be that both groups are equally motivated, in terms of quantity of motivation, but failure or lack of recognition for the middle-class child might only serve to channel his energies more narrowly, while for the lower class child it early becomes dysfunctional, with the effect of converting the original motivation into a rejection of intellectual striving.

EFFECTS OF SCHOOL FAILURE ON THE CHILD

Failure in school for the middle-class child can be more personally disorganizing because the continuity of values from home to school ensures that such a child will be considered a failure in both places. However, as was already pointed out, there are also more resources available for helping the child to cope with the failure and to recover from it, and to mitigate its degree.

For the lower class child, school failure may result in less personal upset or disturbance but may be more final, both in terms of recovery of adequate functioning in school and in terms of occupational choices. Such failure may have the result of gradually but nevertheless effectively alienating the child from the school and the structure of opportunity which is associated with it.

In addition, though these parents may or may not be opposed to the specific act involved in the child's leaving school prematurely, they may have shared with the child their own personal affect regarding their experiences with social institutions. Particularly the minority group lower-class parent is likely to explain, rationalize, and attribute job and economic frustration—both correctly and incorrectly—to the operation of impersonal societal institutions. He may thus identify, accurately and inaccurately, these same institutions with his child's experience in school. This negative affect can rapidly and perhaps inadvertently be generalized to the whole school learning process.

This kind of constellation has particular significance where the school system operates as a bureaucratic mechanism, isolated from the community, and unable to counteract the consequences of inadequate preparation for functioning in the school factory. So the school, at the time the child decides to leave it, has little influence with either the child or the parent, and even if it did, it is frequently just not programmed for interpreting process to non-middle-class children and adults.

ALIENATION OR INCREASING RAPPORT?

Thus, if the school is to influence the continued attendance of children, the influence must begin and the channels for its transmission must be opened well before the school failure and the dropout problem arise.[2] This brings us to the first

[2] Of course, not all dropouts are school failures (and there might even be instances when high performance creative children *should* drop out of school —but that would make another paper), but the evidence suggests that the majority are. Similarly, of course, all dropouts are not lower status children, but again the majority are; and I would postulate that with middle-class children there is a higher incidence among dropouts of psychological malfunctioning, while with lower status children it is more likely to be associated with sociocognitive dissonance and general problems of communication.

contact of the child and his parents with the school. The
process of alienation or, on the other hand, of increasing rap-
port, begins here. It is at this level that certain crucial questions must be asked.

First, is the child intellectually and psychologically ready
for the school experience, for the specific curriculum, and for
the demands of comprehension, communication, motor control, and timing made by the school? The reference here is not
to specific "readiness" as the term as been characteristically
used in educational circles but, rather, to the sociocognitive
preparations and anticipations of the child for this new experience. Next, are the parents helped to become aware of the
school purpose, the nature of its demands on the child, and
how they—even if uneducated—can play a meaningful role in
the education of their child? Is the school accessible to these
parents? In other words, is it a place which stimulates embar-
rassment for their ignorance and fear of its power, or is it a
center for comfortable contact and a sharing of their interest
in their child?

In this interaction among three elements, what about the
school itself—the third element? Is it a structure that the community can be proud of, and where staff can share this pride?
Do its teachers and administrators see a challenge, or are they
interested only in securing discipline and in surviving the
day? Do they have some understanding of the social backgrounds of their children, the temporary limitations that
might have been imposed by these backgrounds (in terms of
good schoolwork)? Is there a reasonable amount of staff
stability, particularly in the early years? And is there some
attempt to adjust the curriculum and primers to current life
realities?

The answers to these questions we all really know. The experiences of the child from the disadvantaged background
simply do not prepare him for successful school performance.

The teacher has, more often than not, *not* been trained in the sociology of learning, and also, more often than not, her training fails to give her a sense of challenge in teaching children, particularly those who start out with handicaps. Usually she prefers—both by training and personal inclination—the immediately bright, responsive child who also most probably places a type of demand on her professional skills which is more congruent with the orientation of her training.

The schools are more likely than not to be underequipped, closed to the children for after-school experimentation with extracurricular books and arts and crafts, and closed to the community as evening centers for learning and socializing. More likely than not, nobody explains to the parents how they can help or be important factors in the education of their child, and the whole process of their child's education—even for the few who become active in the PTA's—remains foreign and alien, and often their contact with the school carries a condescending quality. The early curriculum is likely to be unfamiliar, experientially discontinuous, while the primer, despite all criticism, is still most likely to be boring, repetitious, suburban, and altogether too white.

What we have stated here, of course, are some of the major problems of getting a grip on children from social and cultural backgrounds which do not participate in the middle-class values of the school. These problems are raised here not because it is now fashionable to lay at their door all of our current social difficulties, but because to me it is inconceivable to consider the problem of the high school dropout without focusing on the early relationship among the child, the family, and the school, and the transition between the preschool environment and the school.

Considering all these combinations, factors, and circumstances, it is amazing that as many children as do still find sufficient relevance in the school experience to remain. In this context it might be noted parenthetically that the real occupational expectations of these children are more congruent with their homes and community experiences than they are with the school setting. It might be that only as school is perceived as being more functionally relevant to adult occupations can early negative experiences become decreasingly influential in the decision to leave school. Here is not meant the Conant solution of simply more vocational high schools but, rather, the *same opportunity distribution for all populations,* regardless of subgroup membership.

IMPORTANCE OF A PRE-SCHOOL TRAINING PROGRAM

There are many possible avenues through which solutions for these problems might be evolved. But none of them exists independently, and any successful solution would have to involve a confluence of institutional changes on the level of the child, of the curriculum, of teacher preparation, adequate economic school support, and community-school bridges with twoway traffic. Nevertheless, there are certain possibilities for social intervention on the child-focused level that may open individual escape hatches and that might require minimal structural and process change in the current school operation. The most important of these areas of social intervention, and one that comes least into conflict with existing institutionalized barricades to change, would be that of an intensive, highly focused, pre-school training program.

There are no data at the present time to prove that a pre-school program could reduce the incidence of later dropout (though such data would not be difficult to collect), so this paper must be considered a speculative discussion. We have some preliminary data on this which indicate that pre-school, kindergarten, or day-care experience, or a combination of these, is associated with higher group intelligence test scores. The scores are higher in the first grade, and the differential tends to be accentuated in a fifth grade population; apparently this differential holds when social class is controlled.[3]

From present data it cannot be said definitely that there is any direct relationship between the early school experience and the school dropout, but I would hypothesize a very strong relationship between the first school experiences of the child and academic success or failure, and that the more invariant the school experience, the more important the early experience would be to the academic success of the child. I would also hypothesize that children who have had a pre-school and kindergarten experience are more likely to cope appropriately with the kinds of things the school demands intellectually than are children who have not had this experience. This would be particularly true for children from lower socioeconomic groups, and would be most true for children who come from the most peripheral groups in our society.

For example, what happens when a child from these groups comes to school for the first time in the first grade? If he has not had experience with books; with the kinds of perceptual and developmental demands that are made by the school; with the kinds of language demands implicit in the nature of the communication that comes from the teacher to the child? That child's chances of starting to fail within the school situation are greatly enhanced. It is common in the first grade for a teacher to talk to the class for a period of ten minutes or so. Yet very often these children have never before experienced a ten-minute-long speech sequence coming from an adult to a child. So, in school, at the very beginning the child experiences this "foreign" information coming in at a rapid rate, requiring complex auditory differentiations for which life has not programmed him.

What is likely to happen in this process, and fairly imme-

3 These data, which are currently being analyzed, were gathered by the Institute for Developmental Studies and will be separately reported as part of a larger study.

diately, is that the child will start to look upon school as a place where he doesn't understand and where he experiences much failure. Perhaps more important, the teacher often starts to build in expectations of the child's failing. It is likely that at a very early age, the child perceives this expectation of failure. And the children who are most likely to have these expectations directed toward them are children who come with the fewest aptitudes for a middle-class-life-oriented situation. They are likely to be the most poorly dressed, to have a dialect, to come to school somewhat late, and, in general, are likely not to fit naturally into the kinds of middle-class strictures and constrictions that are established within the school system.

The child who comes to school with very few of the kinds of intellectual cognitive structures that school demands will be basically the most susceptible to this process of failing and will be the least likely to start communicating with the teacher. The critical question, then, is whether a child can at least start the educational process by learning the basic skills. In order to accomplish this for children from socially marginal backgrounds, I would say that some kind of antecedent experience that would compensate for the inadequacies within the home and in the social structure would be very beneficial and would be likely to help the child to achieve a positive adjustment to the demands of the school. (The use of the term "adjustment" here is not meant to imply adjustment to the social aspects of the school process or to the conformity pressures of the school—those questions are beyond the scope of this paper.)

A good pre-school program would attempt to give the child the antecedent preparations for school that the home, community, and at least relative affluence give to the middle-class child. Such programs could be set up only after intensive training of teachers and staff to work on the problems of communicating with the parents as well as developing methods and techniques for compensating the child for a narrowness of experiential variation. The attempt would be to enrich those developmental areas most functional and operative in the school learning situation, thereby establishing both cognitive and attitudinal continuity between the pre-school and the school years. Hopefully, knowing that the child is most responsive to acquiring basic skills in the pre-school and early school years, these skills can be fostered, and their acquisition can thus help lay the basis for a reduction in school failure experiences and an increase in school success.

The skills referred to here would include, for example, the visual and auditory perception which underlie reading, language skills, spatial and temporal orientation, general information, familiarity with books, toys, games, and the development of a sustained curiosity. In addition, the attempt must be made to engage the child as an active participant in the learning process rather than as a passive recipient of a school experience.

Establishing a good base. In facilitating the learning process in these children, the school must expect frequently to do a portion of the job traditionally assigned to the home, and curriculum must be reorganized to provide for establishing a good base.

The child, from the time he enters school and is exposed to assumptions about him derived from experience with the middle-class child, has few success experiences and much failure and generalized frustration. The frustration inherent in not understanding, not succeeding, and not being stimulated in the school, while being regulated by it, creates a basis for the further development of negative self-images and low evaluations of individual competencies.

It is important to emphasize that the early training to counteract this process is not a matter of inculcating middle-class values but, rather, of reinforcing the development of those underlying skills that are operationally appropriate and necessary for both successful and psychologically pleasant school learning experiences. The fact that these skills are almost routinely stimulated in middle-class homes does not mean that in content they are middle class: for example, there is nothing fundamentally culturally loaded in a good or poor memory, but it can be awfully important in preparing for an examination.

Interpreting an appropriate behavior. Another question must be considered, and that is how the child's first anticipations are developed toward the school. It is often stated that among Negro parents there is low motivation toward school accomplishment. I have not found this so: I found a great degree of motivation, but a lack of understanding of how instrumentally to make this operative for the child. The problem, then, is to interpret for the child the kind of behavior that will make it possible to function and cope with the school mechanisms.

One way this could be handled is through a direct relationship between the teacher and the community. For example, there are some communities where the school is seen as the resource center—where it is kept open in the evening; there are library books that can be taken out; and where generally there is an attempt to have the school seen as a place of social transition. When the school is a real part of his life and of his community, the child can more normally have the opportunity someday to decide if he wishes to go toward a learning experience consistent with the demands of the school, if he wants to stop off with a lower level of education, or if he wishes to go toward advancement in some other type of vocation with skills less closely related to the formal school demands.

To return more directly to the problem of anticipations toward the school, I do think that the sense of failure that often develops at an early stage projects itself through the total experiences of the child, not only temporally, in terms of his reaction to the demands of the school, but also in terms of his whole concept of self-identification, of a positive self-concept, of the development of a sense of dignity. This sense of dignity, I think, is closely related to how much money, how much concern, how much institutional modification we are willing to put into the school. In neighborhoods where most schools have practically every window broken, there are some protected schools which are beautifully kept: there is a reciprocal feedback, as if the institution and the children were working and co-operating with one another—and there is a sense of mutual respect that goes along with it. Here too, of course, is where teacher training in community sociology and mental health becomes a very important question.

Developing the child's inner self. Horizons and goals are stimulated early in life, and if the parents have had low ceilings in terms of variety of experiences, with the intensity being in terms of job insecurity, negotiations with welfare and landlords, and the like, there is not much left to give the child a sense of identifying the self with goals that take individual impetus and disciplining. This problem, in a larger context, is societal, and has its analogous aspects in the routinized existence of middle-class suburbia, rigid schedules, automated work, and cities and suburbs that share a sameness and drabness. Sometimes the excitement to be sparked in a child must reach his subjective self, his imagination and individual poetry. After this, he might make discriminations and differentiations not seen by his peers in the external world. This development of the inner self can certainly start soon after the development of language, and can be an intrinsic part of the pre-school experience, and possibly a basis for much later motivation.

PROSPECTS FOR A PRE-SCHOOL PROGRAM

The emphasis in this paper on the pre-school program as a means of accommodation between the school and the child and his family represents, it is felt, a necessary approach to the dropout problem. It is beyond the scope of this paper to examine it from the other end of the continuum: the problem of the motivation of the high school student to join the labor force when the opportunities available to him may not be numerous or productive. Further, the high incidence of minority group dropouts makes necessary a consideration of prejudice in employment patterns. But these are broad societal problems, to be attacked and solved in the social arena. And if they were solved, the individual problems of the unprepared child coming into the unpreparing school would assume even greater importance. Developmentally, it would seem that this is one of the first areas in which to approach the problem, and one for which there may be less resistance.

There seems to be great need in mid-twentieth-century America thoroughly to discuss all problems, investigate their causes, delineate possible solutions, and implement only those solutions that have been sufficiently skeletonized so that they no longer represent threats to the status quo. The danger to the approach discussed here is that it will be put into the context of the stress-free, quasi-"purposeful" play, psychologically supportive, momistically oriented, de-intellectualized, sterile enclosures where much of early childhood education is located. If such takes place, social experimentation in this area could have the fate previously indicated. But if the social scientists and educators undertake such a project jointly in a spirit of experimentation and with joint determination to kill the accumulated sacred cows, the possibilities of success are greatly enhanced.

3. The Psychological Basis for Using Pre-School Enrichment as an Antidote for Cultural Deprivation

J. McVicker Hunt[1]

It is very interesting, and very exciting for me, to encounter people who are generally considered sensible, planning to utilize pre-school experiences as an antidote for what we are now calling cultural deprivation and social disadvantage. The group at the Child Welfare Research Station in Iowa, under George D. Stoddard (see Stoddard and Wellman, 1940), described effects of nursery school which they considered evidence that would justify just such a use of nursery schools. This was about twenty-five years ago. Their work, however, was picked to pieces by critics and in the process lost much of the suggestive value it was justified in having. Many of you will recall the ridicule that was heaped upon the "wandering IQ" (Simpson, 1939) and the way in which such people as Florence Goodenough (1939) derided in print the idea of a group of thirteen "feeble-minded" infants being brought within the range of normal mentality through training by moron nursemaids in an institution for the feebleminded (re-

[1] J. McVicker Hunt is a member of the Department of Psychology at the University of Illinois. This article was prepared for the Arden House Conference on Pre-School Enrichment of Socially Disadvantaged Children (December 1962) and appeared in the *Merrill-Palmer Quarterly of Behavior and Development*, Volume 10, Number 3, July 1964.

ferring to the work of Skeels and Dye, 1939, to which we shall return). The fact that just such a use of pre-school experience is now being seriously planned by sensible people with widespread approval means that something has changed.

The change, of course, is not in the nature of man or in the nature of his development; it is rather in our conceptions of man's nature and of his development. Some of our most important beliefs about man and his development have changed or are in the process of changing. It is these changes in belief which have freed us to try as demonstrative experiments what only as recently as World War II would have been considered a stupid waste of effort and time. It is also these changes in theoretical belief about man and his development which provide my topic, namely, the psychological basis for using pre-school enrichment as an antidote for cultural deprivation.

I number these changed or changing beliefs as six. Let me state them in their pre-change form; in the form, in other words, that has so much hampered the sort of enterprise in which this group is about to engage:

(1) a belief in fixed intelligence;

(2) a belief in predetermined development;

(3) a belief in the fixed and static, telephone-switchboard nature of brain function;

(4) a belief that experience during the early years, and particularly before the development of speech, is unimportant;

(5) a belief that whatever experience does affect later development is a matter of emotional reactions based on the fate of instinctual needs;

(6) a belief that learning must be motivated by homeostatic need, by painful stimulation, or by acquired drives based on these.

THE BELIEF IN FIXED INTELLIGENCE

Almost every idea has roots in a communicated conceptual history and in observed evidence. The notion of fixed intelligence has conceptual roots in Darwin's (1859) theory of evolution and in the intense emotional controversy that surrounded it. You will recall that Darwin believed that evolution took place, not by changes wrought through use or disuse as Lamarck (1809) had thought, but by changes resulting from variations in the progeny of every species or strain which are then selected by the conditions under which they live. Their selection is a matter of which variations survive to reproduce so that the variations are passed on into the successive generations. The change is conceived thus to be one that comes via the survival of a variation in a strain through reproduction. Implicit in this notion was the assumption that the characteristics of any organism are predetermined by the genetic constitution with which the organism comes into being as a fertilized ovum. Probably this implicit assumption would never have caught on with anywhere near the force it did, had it not been for two outstanding figures in the history of relatively recent thought. The first of these is Sir Francis Galton, Charles Darwin's younger cousin. You will remember that it was Galton who made the assumption of the hereditary determination of adult characteristics explicit. Galton reasoned, furthermore, that if his cousin were correct, it would mean that the hope of improving the lot of man does not lie in *euthenics*, or in trying to change him through education; rather, such hope lies in *eugenics*, or in the selection of those superior persons who should survive. Secondly, he saw that if decisions were to be made as to which human beings were to survive and reproduce, it would be necessary to have some criteria for survival. So he founded his anthropometric laboratory for the measurement of man, with the hope that by means of tests he could determine those individuals who should survive. Note that he was not deciding merely who should be selected for jobs in a given industry, but who should survive to reproduce. This was his concern. Because of the abhorrence which such a plan met, Galton talked and wrote relatively little about it. However, the combination of the context of his lifework with the few remarks he did make on the subject gives these remarks convincing significance (see Hunt, 1961).

Galton had a pupil who was very influential in bringing such conceptions into the stream of American thought. This was J. McKeen Cattell, who brought Galton's tests to America and, beginning in 1890, gave them to college students, first at the University of Pennsylvania and then at Columbia University. Because Cattell was also an influential teacher at both Penn and Columbia, his influence spread through the many students he had before World War I—when his sympathies with Germany led to a painful separation from Columbia.

A second psychologist who was almost equally influential in bringing the stream of thought supporting fixed intelligence into American thought is G. Stanley Hall. Hall did not personally know Galton; neither did he personally know Darwin, but he read about evolution while still a college student, and, as he has written in his autobiography, "it struck me like a light; this was the thing for me." Hall's importance lies in that he communicated a strong attachment to the notion of fixed intelligence to his students at Clark University, of which he was the first President, and these students became leaders of the new psychology in America. Among them were three of the most illustrious leaders of the testing movement. One was Henry H. Goddard, who first translated the Binet tests into English for use at the Vineland Training School and also wrote the story of the Kallikak family (1912). Another was F. Kuhlman, who was also an early translator and reviser of the Binet tests and who, with Rose G. Anderson, adapted them for use with pre-school children. The third was Lewis

Terman, who is the author of the Stanford-Binet revision, the most widely known version of the Binet tests in America. These three communicated their faith in fixed intelligence to a major share of those who spread the testing movement in America.

So much for the conceptual roots of the belief in fixed intelligence that come by way of communication in the history of thought.

The assumption of fixed intelligence also had an empirical basis. Not only did test-retest reliabilities show that the positions of individuals in a group remained fairly constant, but also the tests showed some capacity to predict such criterion performances as school success, success as officers in World War I, etc. All such evidence concerned children of school age for whom the experience to which they are exposed is at least to some degree standardized (see Hunt, 1961). When investigators began to examine the constancy of the DQ (developmental quotient) or IQ in pre-school children, the degree of constancy proved to be very much lower. You will recall some of the very interesting interpretations of this lack of constancy in the pre-school DQ (see Hunt, 1961, pp. 311 ff). Anderson argued that since the tests at successive ages involved different functions, constancy could not be expected. But an epigenesis of man's intellectual functions is inherent in the nature of his development, and the implications of this fact were apparently missed by these critics of the findings from the infant tests. While they knew that the basic structure of intelligence changes in its early phases of development just as the structures of the body change in the embryological phase of morphological development, they appear not to have noted that it is thus inevitable that the infant tests must involve differing content and functions at successive ages.

It was Woodworth (1941) who argued, after examining the evidence from the studies of twins, that there might be some difference in IQ due to the environment but that which exists among individuals in our culture is largely due to the genes. In the context of cultural deprivation, I believe Woodworth asked the wrong question. He might better have asked: What would be the difference in the IQ of a pair of identical twins at age six if one were reared as Myrtle McGraw (1935) reared the trained twin, Johnny (so that he was swimming at four months, rollerskating at eleven months, and developing various such skills at about one half to one fourth the age that people usually develop them), and if the other twin were reared in an orphanage, like the one described by Wayne Dennis (1960) in Teheran, where 60 per cent of the infants two years of age are still not sitting up alone and where 85 per cent of those four years of age are still not walking alone? While observations of this kind come from varied sources and lack the force of controlled experimentation, they suggest strongly that lack of constancy is the rule for either IQ or DQ during the pre-school years and that the IQ is not at all fixed unless the culture or the school fixes the program of environmental encounters. Cross-sectional validity may be substantial, with predictive validity being little above zero (see Hunt, 1961). In fact, trying to predict what the IQ of an individual child will be at age eighteen from a DQ obtained during his first or second year is much like trying to predict how fast a feather might fall in a hurricane. The law of falling bodies holds only under the specified and controlled conditions of a vacuum. Similarly, any laws concerning the rate of intellectual growth must take into account the series of environmental encounters which constitute the conditions of that growth.

THE BELIEF IN PREDETERMINED DEVELOPMENT

The belief in predetermined development has been no less hampering, for a serious consideration of pre-school enrichment as an antidote for cultural deprivation than that in fixed intelligence. This belief also has historical roots in Darwin's theory of evolution. It got communicated into the mainstream of psychological thought about development by G. Stanley Hall (see Pruette, 1926). Hall gave special emphasis to the belief in predetermined development by making central in his version of the theory of evolution the conception of recapitulation. This is the notion that the development of an individual shows in summary form the development of the species. It was Arnold Gesell, another student of G. Stanley Hall, whose life's work concerned the normative description of children's behavioral development. Gesell took over Hall's faith in predetermined development in his own notion that development is governed by what he has termed "intrinsic growth." It should be noted that once one believes in "intrinsic growth," the normative picture of development is not only a description of the process but an explanation of it as well. Thus, whenever little Johnny does something "bad," the behavior can be explained by noting that it is just a stage he is going through. Moreover, following Hall's parable of the tadpole's tail—in which the hind legs fail to develop if the tail is amputated—Johnny's unwanted behavior must not be hampered else some desirable future characteristic will fail to appear.

This notion of predetermined development also has an empirical basis, for the evidence from various early studies of behavioral development in both lower animals and children was readily seen as consonant with it. Among these are Coghill's (1929) studies of behavioral development in amblystoma. These demonstrated that behavioral development, like anatomical development, starts at the head end and proceeds tailward, starts from the inside and proceeds outward, and consists of a progressive differentiation of more specific units from general units. From such evidence Coghill and others inferred the special additional notion that behavior unfolds automatically as the anatomical basis for behavior matures.

From such a background came the differentiation of the process of learning from the process of maturation.

Among the early studies of behavioral development are those of Carmichael (1926, 1927, 1928), also with amblystoma and frogs, which appeared to show that the circumstances in which development takes place are of little consequence. You will recall that Carmichael divided batches of amblystoma and frog eggs. One of these batches he chloretoned to inhibit their activity; another batch he kept in tap water on an ordinary table; and a third group he kept in tap water on a workbench, where they received extra stimulation. Those kept in tap water on an ordinary table swam as early as did those that got the extra stimulation from the workbench. Moreover, even though those that were chloretoned had been prevented from activity through five days, they appeared to be as adept at swimming within a half an hour after the chloretone was washed out as were either of the two batches reared in tap water. Although Carmichael himself was very careful in interpreting these results, they have commonly been interpreted to mean that development is almost entirely a function of maturation and that learning, as represented in practice, is of little consequence.

Such an interpretation got further support from early studies of the effects of practice. In one such study of a pair of identical twins by Gesell and Thompson (1929), the untrained twin became as adept at tower-building and stair-climbing after a week of practice as was the trained twin who had been given practice in tower-building and stair-climbing over many weeks. In another such study by Josephine Hilgard (1932), a group of ten pre-school children were given practice cutting with scissors, climbing a ladder, and buttoning over a period of twelve weeks; yet they retained their superiority over the control group, which had received no special practice, for only a very short time. One week of practice in those skills by the control group brought their performance up to a level which was no longer significantly inferior to that of the experimental group from a statistical standpoint. Later work by two other investigators appeared to lend further support. Dennis and Dennis (1940) found that the children of Hopi Indians raised on cradleboards, which inhibited the movements of their legs and arms during waking hours, walked at the same age as did Hopi children reared freely, in the typical white man's manner. Moreover, Dennis and Dennis (1935, 1938, 1941) found the usual sequence of autogenic behavior items in a pair of fraternal twins reared under conditions of "restricted practice and minimal social stimulation." Many such studies appeared to yield results which could be readily seen as consonant with the notion that practice has little effect on the rate of development, and that the amount of effect to be got from practice is a function of the level of maturation present when the practice occurs.

It was just such a notion and just such evidence that led Watson (1928) to argue in his book, *The Psychological Care of the Infant and Child*, that experience is unimportant during the pre-school years because nothing useful can be learned until the child has matured sufficiently. Thus, he advised that the best thing possible is to leave the child alone to grow. Then, when the child has "lain and grown," when the response repertoire has properly matured, those in charge of his care can introduce learning. He conceived that learning could "get in its licks" tying these responses to proper stimuli, via the conditioning principle, and by linking them together in chains to produce complex skills. I suspect that the use of B. F. Skinner's baby-box, with controlled temperature, humidity, etc., may be based upon just such assumptions of predetermined development and of an automatic unfolding of a basic behavioral repertoire with anatomical maturation.

It should be noted that the animal evidence cited here comes from amblystoma and frogs, which are well down the phylogenetic scale. They have brains in which the ratio of those portions concerned with association or intrinsic processes to the portions concerned directly with input and output is small; that is, the A/S (Association/Stimulus) ratio, as formulated by Hebb (1949), is small. When organisms with higher A/S ratios were studied, in somewhat the fashion in which Coghill and Carmichael studied the behavioral development of amblystoma and frogs, the evidence yielded has been highly dissonant with the implications of predetermined development. When Cruze (1935, 1938) found that the number of pecking errors per twenty-five trials decreased through the first five days, even though the chicks were kept in the dark—a result consonant with the notion of predeterminism— he also found facts pointing in a contrary direction. For instance, chicks kept in the dark for twenty consecutive days, and given an opportunity to see light and have pecking-experience only during the daily tests, *failed* to attain a high level of accuracy in pecking and exhibited almost no improvement in the striking-seizing-swallowing sequence.

Similarly, Kuo's (see Hunt, 1961) wonderful behavioral observations on the embryological development of chicks in the egg indicate that the responses comprising the pecking and locomotor patterns have been "well practiced" long before hatching. The "practice" for pecking seems to start with head-bobbing, which is among the first embryonic movements to be observed. The practice for the locomotor patterns begins with vibratory motions of the wing-buds and leg-buds; these movements become flexion and extension as the limbs lengthen and joints appear. At about the eleventh day of incubation, the yolk sac characteristically moves over to the ventral side of the embryo. This movement of the yolk sac forces the legs to fold on the breast and to be held there. From this point on, the legs cannot be fully extended. They are forced henceforth to hatching to remain in this folded position with extensive thrusts only against the yolk sac. Kuo argues that this condition establishes a fixed resting posture for the legs, and prepares them for lifting of the chick's body in standing and locomotion. Moreover, his interpretation gets some support from "an experiment of nature." In the seven thousand embryos that he observed, nearly two hundred crippled chicks appeared. These crippled chicks could neither stand nor walk after hatching. Neither could they sit in the roosting position, because their legs were deformed. Over 80 per cent of those with deformed legs occurred in those instances in which the yolk sac failed for some reason, still unknown, to move over to the ventral side of the embryo.

Such observations suggest that the mammalian advent of increasingly long uterine control of embryological and fetal environment in phylogeny reflects the fact that environmental circumstances more and more become important for early development, as the central nervous system control becomes more predominant. It should be noted, moreover, that as central nervous system control becomes more predominant, capacity for regeneration decreases. Perhaps this implies a waning of the relative potency of the chemical predeterminers of development as one goes up the phylogenetic scale.

Perhaps even more exciting in this connection is the work of Austin Riesen (1958), Brattgård (1952), and others. Riesen undertook the rearing of chimpanzees in darkness in order to test some of Hebb's (1949) hypotheses of the importance of primary learning in the development of perception. What he appears to have discovered—along with Brattgård (1952); Liberman (1962); Rasch, Swift, Riesen, and Chow (1961); and Weiskrantz (1958)—is that even certain anatomical structures of the retina require light stimulation for proper development. The chimpanzee babies who were kept in the dark for a year and a half have atypical retinas; and, even after they are brought into the light, the subsequent development of their retinas goes awry and they become permanently blind. The result of such prolonged stimulus deprivation during infancy appears to be an irreversible process that does not occur when the chimpanzee infant is kept in darkness for only something like seven months. Inasmuch as Weiskrantz (1958) has found a scarcity of Müller fibers in the retinas of kittens reared in the dark, and since other investigators (especially Brattgård, 1952) have found the retinal-ganglion cells of animals reared in the dark to be deficient in the production of ribonucleic acid (RNA), these studies of rearing under conditions of sensory deprivation appear to be lending support to Hydén's (1959, 1960) hypothesis. This reasons that the effects of experience may be stored as RNA within the glial component of retinal tissue and, perhaps, of brain tissue as well.

For our present purposes, it is enough to note that such studies are bringing evidence that even the anatomical structures of the central nervous system are affected in their development by experience. This lends credence to Piaget's (1936) aphorism that "use is the aliment of a schema."

Consider another study of the effects of early experience. This is a study by Thompson and Heron (1954), comparing the adult problem-solving ability of Scotty pups which were reared as pets in human homes from the time of weaning until they were eight months of age with that of their litter-mates reared in isolation in laboratory cages for the same period. The adult tests were made when the animals were eighteen months old, after they had been together in the dog pasture for a period of ten months. Adult problem-solving was measured by means of the Hebb-Williams (1946) test of animal intelligence. In one of these tests, the dog is brought into a room while hungry. After being allowed to smell and see a bowl of food, the dog is permitted to watch as this food is removed and put behind a screen in one of the opposite corners of the room. Both pet-reared and cage-reared dogs go immediately to the spot where the food disappeared. After the same procedure has been repeated several times, the food is then placed, while the animal watches, behind a screen in another opposite corner of the room. In order to see this clearly, think of the first screen being in the corner to the dog's right, the second in the corner to the dog's left. Now, when the dog is released, if he is pet-reared he goes immediately to the screen in the left corner for food. But, if he was cage-reared, he is more likely to go to the screen in the right corner where he had previously found food. In his tests of object permanence, Piaget (1936) describes behavior of children about nine months old resembling that of the cage-reared pups, and of children about fourteen months old resembling that of the pet-reared pups.

It is interesting to compare the results of this study by Thompson and Heron (1954), in which dogs were the subjects, with the results of various studies of the effects of early experiences on adult problem-solving in which rats were subjects (see Hebb, 1947; Gauron and Becker, 1959; Wolf, 1943). Whereas the effects of early experience on the problem-solving of dogs appear to be both large and persistent, they appear to be both less marked and less permanent in the rat. Such a comparison lends further credence to the proposition that the importance of the effects of early experience increases as the associative or intrinsic portions of the cerebrum increase in proportion, as reflected in Hebb's notion of the A/S ratio.

But what about the fact that practice appears to have little or no effect on the development of a skill in young children? How can one square the absence of the effects of practice with the tremendous apathy and retardation commonly to be found in children reared in orphanages? In the case of the orphanage in Teheran reported on by Dennis (1960), the retardation in locomotor function is so great, as I have already noted, that 60 per cent fail to sit up alone at two years of age, even though nearly all children ordinarily sit up at ten months of age; and 85 per cent still fail to walk alone at four years of age, even though children typically walk at about fourteen or fifteen months of age and nearly all are walking before they are two years of age. I believe the two sets of results can be squared by taking into account the epigenesis in the structure of behavior that occurs during the earliest years. The investigators of the effects of practice neglected this epigenesis. They sought the effects of experience only in practice of the function or schema to be observed and measured. The existence of an epigenesis of intellectual function implies that the experiential roots of a given schema will lie in antecedent activities quite different in structure from the schema to be observed and measured. Thus, antecedent practice at tower-building and buttoning may be relatively unimportant for the development of skill in these activities; but an unhampered antecedent opportunity to throw objects and to manipulate them in a variety of situations, and an even earlier opportunity to have seen a variety of sights and to have heard a variety of sounds, may be of tremendous importance in determining both the age at which tower-building and buttoning will occur and the degree of skill that the child will manifest. I shall return to this topic.

BRAIN FUNCTION CONCEIVED AS A STATIC SWITCHBOARD

One can not blame Darwin for the conception of brain function as static, like that in a telephone switchboard. The origin of the ferment leading to these conceptions, however, does derive from Darwin's (1872) shift of attention from the evolution of the body to the evolution of mind. This he began in his book, *The Expressions of the Emotions in Man and Animals*. It was thus Darwin who provided the stimulus for what was later to be called *comparative psychology*. The original purpose was to show that there is a gradual transition from the lower animals to man in the various faculties of mind. It was Romanes (1882, 1883) who took up this task in an attempt to show the manner in which intelligence has evolved. Romanes' method was to show through anecdotes that animals are capable of intelligent behavior, albeit at a level of complexity inferior to man's. It was C. Lloyd Morgan (1894) who said that it was reasoning by very loose analogy to impute to dogs, cats, and the like, the same kind of conscious processes and faculties that man can report. Then, shortly, Thorndike and Woodworth (1901) knocked out such old-fashioned faculties as memory with their studies showing that such forms of practice as daily memorizing poetry does not improve a person's capacity to memorize other types of material, and that being taught mathematics and Latin does not improve performance on reasoning tests.

It was still obvious, however, that animals do learn and that they do solve problems. Morgan (1894) saw this occurring by a process of trial and error. According to this conception, as Hull (1943) later elaborated it, an organism comes to any given situation with a ready-made hierarchy of responses. When those at the top of the hierarchy fail to achieve satisfaction, they are supposed to be weakened (extinguished). Other responses lower in the hierarchy then take their places and become connected with stimuli from the situation. Or, as Thorndike (1913) put it earlier, new S-R (Stimulus-Response) bonds are established. Complex behavior was explained by assuming that one response can be the stimulus for another, so that S-R chains could be formed. The role of the brain in such learning also needed explanation. Here the telephone was the dramatic new invention supplying a mechanical model for a conception of the brain's role. Inasmuch as the reflex arc was conceived to be both the anatomical and the functional unit of the nervous system, the role of the brain in learning could readily be conceived to be analogous to that of a telephone switchboard. Thus, the head was emptied of active functions, and the brain, which filled it, came to be viewed as the focus of a variety of static connections.

All this led to what I think is a basic confusion in psychological thought, one which has been prominent for at least the last thirty-five or forty years. This is a confusion between S-R methodology, on the one hand, and S-R theory on the other. We cannot escape S-R methodology. The best one can possibly do empirically is to note the situations in which organisms behave and to observe what they do there. But there is no reason why one should not relate the S-R relationships, the empirical relationships one observes between stimulus and response, to whatever the neurophysiologist can tell us about inner brain function and to whatever the endocrinologist can tell us. The broader one makes his nomological net, the better, in that the more nearly his resulting conceptions will approach those of the imaginary, all-seeing eye of Deity.

Stimulus-Response (S-R) methodology appeared at first to imply the notion of the empty organism. It is interesting to recall, however, that Walter Hunter (1912, 1918) discovered that various animals could delay their responses to stimuli and also learn double alternation. Both achievements implied that there must be some kind of representative or symbolic process intervening between stimulus and response. It was to explain just such behavior, moreover, that Hull (1931) promulgated the notion of the pure-stimulus act. This became in turn the response-produced cues and the response-produced drives of Miller and Dollard. When Miller and Dollard (1941), began conceiving of the responses which serve as stimuli occurring within the brain, traditional S-R theory with its implicit peripherality of both stimulus and response began to fade. The demise of peripheral S-R theory became nearly complete when Osgood (1952) turned these response-produced cues and drives into central mediating processes. It is interesting to note in this connection that it is precisely observations from S-R methodology which have undone traditional peripheral S-R theory, and it is these observations which are now demanding that brain function be conceived in terms of active processes.

The theoretical need for active brain processes, however, has been both stimulated by and got much of its form from cybernetics (Wiener, 1948). Such investigators as Newell, Shaw, and Simon (1958), in the process of programming computers to solve problems, and especially logical problems, have been clarifying the general nature of what is required for solving such problems. They have described three major kinds of requirements: (1) memories or information stored somewhere, and presumably in the brain; (2) operations of a logical sort which are of the order of actions that deal with the information in the memories; and (3) hierarchical arrangements of these operations and memories in programs. Thus, the electronic computer has been replacing the telephone as the mechanical model for brain function.

Such a notion of memories and, even more, the notion of operations of a logical sort as actions, and the notion of hierarchical arrangements of these operations—these notions differ markedly from the notion of reflexes being hitched to each other. Moreover, ablation studies have been showing that it is not communication across the cortex from sensory-input regions to motor-output regions that is important for behavior. The cortex can be diced into very small parts without serious damage to behavioral function; but if the fibers, composed of white matter, under an area of the gray matter cortex are cut, behavior is damaged seriously. Thus, the notion of transcortical association gives way to communication back and forth from the center to the periphery of the brain (see Pribram, 1960). With such changes in conception of brain function being dictated by their own observations, when neuropsychologists become familiar with what is required in programming computers to solve logical problems, it is not surprising that they ask themselves where one might find a locus for the various requirements of computer function—that is, for the memories, the operations, and the hierarchical arrangements of them. Carl Pribram (1960) has reviewed the clinical and experimental findings concerning the functional consequences of injuring various portions of the brain, and he has come up with a provisional answer. The brain appears to be divided into intrinsic portions and extrinsic portions. This is the terminology of Rose and Woolsey (1949), and here the term *intrinsic* is used because this portion has no direct connections with either incoming sensory fibers or outgoing motor fibers. The extrinsic portion is so called because it does have such direct peripheral connections. What Pribram suggests is that these components of what is required for the various kinds of information processing and of decision-making may well reside in these intrinsic portions of the brain.

There are two intrinsic portions: one is the frontal portion of the cortex, with its connections to the dorsal frontal nuclei of the thalamus; the other, the nonsensory portions of the parietal, occipital, and temporal lobes with their connections with the pulvenar or the posterior dorsal nucleus of the thalamus. Injury to the frontal system disrupts executive functions and thereby suggests that it is the locus of the central, neural mechanism for plans. Injury to the posterior intrinsic system results in damage to recognitive functions, which suggests that it may be the locus of central, neural mechanisms for information processing *per se*. The intrinsic portions of the cerebrum appear to become relatively larger and larger as one samples organisms up the phylogenetic scale. Perhaps what Hebb (1949) has called the A/S ratio might better be called the I/E ratio—for "Intrinsic/Extrinsic."

From such studies, one can readily conceive the function of early experience to be one of "programming" these intrinsic portions of the cerebrum so that they can later function effectively in learning and problem-solving.

PREVERBAL EXPERIENCE UNIMPORTANT

Early experience, particularly preverbal experience, however, has historically been considered to be relatively unimportant. It has been argued that such experience can hardly have any effect on adult behavior, because it is not remembered. There have been, of course, a few relatively isolated thinkers who have given at least lip service to the importance of early experience in the development of the personality. Plato is one who thought that the rearing and education of children was too important a function to be carried out by mere amateur parents. But when he described the rearing that children should have in his *Republic,* he described only experiences for youngsters already talking. Rousseau (1762) gave somewhat more than lip service in *Emile* to the importance of early experience. Moreover, at least implicitly, he attributed importance to preverbal experience with his prescription that the child, Emile, should very early be exposed to pain and cold in order that he might be toughened.

An even earlier example is to me somewhat embarrassing. I thought that I had invented the notion of split-litter technique for determining the effects of infant feeding-frustration in rats—but later I found, in reading Plutarch's *Lives,* that Lycurgus, the lawgiver of the Spartans, took puppies from the same litter and reared them in diverse ways, so that some became greedy and mischievous curs while others became followers of the scent and hunters. He exhibited these pups before his contemporaries, saying, "Men of Sparta, of a truth, habit and training and teaching and guidance in living are a great influence toward engendering excellence, and I will make this evident to you at once." Thereupon he produced the dogs with diverse rearing. Perhaps it is from the stories of the Spartans that Rousseau got his notion that Emile should be toughened. Such followers of Rousseau as Pestalozzi and Froebel certainly saw childhood experience as important, but as educators they were concerned with the experiences of children who had already learned to verbalize. So far as I can tell, the notion that preverbal experience is seriously impor-

tant for adult personal characteristics comes from Freud
(1905) and his theory of psychosexual development.

Freud not only attributed importance to preverbal experience; he also proposed an hypothesis concerning the nature
of the kinds of experience important for later development.
These were the experiences deriving from the fate of instinc-
tive impulses arising out of homeostatic need, painful stimulation, and, especially, the pleasure-striving which he saw as
sexual in nature (Freud, 1905). If one examines the objective
studies of the effects of the various kinds of factors deemed to
be important from the standpoint of their theory of psychosexual development, one has a very hard time finding clear
evidence that they are important (see Hunt, 1945, 1956;
Orlansky, 1949). For every study that appears to show an
effect of some given psychosexual factor in early infancy,
there is another study to be matched with it that fails to show
an effect. Furthermore, the more carefully the various studies
appear to be controlled, the more nearly the results tend to
be consonant with the null hypothesis. The upshot of all this
is that it looks very much as if the kinds of factors to which
Freud attributed importance in his theory of psychosexual
development are not very important.

It was commonly believed before World War II that early
experience was important for emotional development and for
the development of personality characteristics, but unimportant for the development of intellect or intelligence. Some of
the animal studies of early experience were widely quoted to
support this belief. One of these was my own study of the effects of infant feeding frustration upon adult hoarding in rats
(Hunt, 1941). Actually, the effects of the infantile feeding
frustration were exhibited in both eating rate and hoarding,
and exhibited in the eating rate more regularly than in the
hoarding. Rats do not always hoard as a consequence of infantile feeding frustration, although they do regularly eat
faster than littermates without such experience. Yet, the feed-

ing or drinking frustration need not occur in infancy to get the effect of speeded eating or speeded drinking (Freedman, 1957). In the case of the work of my colleagues and myself, much of it still unpublished, various kinds of effects that should, theoretically, have followed did not occur. The upshot of all this, I now believe, is that our theoretical expectations were wrong. I also believe that the general notion that the emotional characteristics of persons are most influenced by early experience while the intellectual characteristics are not influenced is also quite wrong.

It now looks as if there may be two quite different kinds of effect of early infantile experience. One is that in which the effect of painful experience is one of reducing the aversiveness of later painful or strange circumstances. The other kind of effect is one increasing the capacity of an organism to learn. Both the shocked rats and the handled rats in the study by Levine, Chevalier, and Korchin (1956) learned to respond to a signal to avoid shock more rapidly than did the rats that remained unmolested in the maternal nest. This is adaptive. Denenberg (1962) has shown that even shocking animals once on the second day of life will decrease the number of trials they require to learn an avoidance response, as compared with those left unmolested in the maternal nest. This kind of effect appears to result not only from shock during the pre-weaning phase of development but also from handling and petting. It looks very much as if any increase in the variation of circumstances encountered during those first three weeks of life will facilitate later learning, not only in the avoidance situation but also in such problem-solving situations as those to be found in the Hebb-Williams (1946) tests of animal intelligence.

Yet another belief about what is important in early experience appears to need correction. G. Stanley Hall was fond of the aphorism that "the mind of man is handmade" (Pruette, 1926). Watson (1919) and the other behaviorists have believed that it is the motor side, rather than the sensory side, that is important in learning. Dewey (1902) gave emphasis to the motor side also in his belief that the child learns chiefly by doing. Dewey went even further to emphasize that the things that the child should be encouraged to do are the things that he would later be called upon to do in taking his place in society. More recently, Osgood (1952) has conceived that the central processes which mediate meanings are the residues of past responses. I am simply trying to document my assertion that in the dominant theory of the origin of mind or of central mediating processes, these have been conceived to be based upon the residues from past responses.

Hebb's (1949) theorizing, as I have already noted, took sharp issue with this dominant theoretical position. He has conceived the basis for primary learning to be chiefly on the sensory side. Riesen (1958) began his experiments on the effects of rearing chimpanzees in darkness with what he called S-S, or stimulus-stimulus relations. Piaget (1936), although he has emphasized "activity as the aliment of a schema," has conceived of *looking* and *listening,* both of which are typically viewed as sensory input channels, as existing among the schemata ready-made at birth. Moreover, it is looking and listening to which he attributes key importance during the first phases of intellectual development. This emphasis is registered in his aphorism that, "the more a child has seen and heard, the more he wants to see and hear" (Piaget, 1936).

Evidence requiring this correction of belief come from more than just the studies of the effects of early perceptual experience on the later problem-solving capacity of animals. It also comes from comparing the effects of the cradling practice on the age of onset of walking in Hopi children, with the effects of the homogeneous auditory and visual stimulation on the age of onset of walking in the children in a Teheran orphanage. The cradling practice inhibits actions of an infant's legs and arms during his waking hours through most of the first year of his life. Yet, the mean and standard deviation of the age of walking for those cradled proved to be the same as that for those Hopi children reared with free use of their legs and arms (Dennis and Dennis, 1940). Contrariwise, 85 per cent of the children in the Teheran orphanage were still not walking alone at four years of age—and here the factor in which the circumstances of these children most differ from those of most young infants was probably the continuous homogeneity of auditory and visual experience (Dennis, 1960). The children of the Teheran orphanage had full use of the motor function of their legs and arms. The Hopi children reared with the cradling practice did not have free use of their legs and arms —but they were exposed, by virtue of their being carried around on their mothers' backs, to a very rich variety of auditory and visual inputs.

Perhaps this emphasis on the motor side is erroneous only as another example of failure to take into account the epigenesis of behavioral and intellectual functions. While it may be true that education by doing is best for children of kindergarten and primary school age, it appears that having a variety of things to listen to and look at may be most important for development during the first year of life (see also Fiske and Maddi, 1961).

ALL BEHAVIOR AND ALL LEARNING IS MOTIVATED BY PAINFUL STIMULATION OR HOMEOSTATIC NEED

The fact that both apathy and retardation have been regularly noted in orphanage-reared children who typically live under conditions of homogeneous circumstances (especially marked of the children observed by Dennis in the Teheran orphanage) suggests that homogeneous stimulation somehow reduces motivation. This suggestion brings me to yet another major change of theoretical belief.

It is common to state that "all behavior is motivated." But to make this statement specific, it must be completed with the complex phrase, "by homeostatic need, painful stimulation, or by innocuous stimuli which have previously been associated with these." This has been the dominant conception of motivation for most of the last half century—dominant because it has been held both by academic behavior theorists (e.g., Dashiell, 1928; Holt, 1931; Freeman, 1934; Guthrie, 1938; Melton, 1941; Miller and Dollard, 1941; Hull, 1943; Mowrer, 1960) and by psychoanalysts (e.g., Freud, 1915; Fenichel, 1945).

This notion implies that organisms should become quiescent in the absence of painful stimulation, homeostatic need, or the acquired drives based upon them. Since World War II, evidence has accumulated to indicate quite clearly that neither animals nor children actually do become quiescent in the absence of such motivating conditions (see Hunt, 1963a). Bühler (1928) noted earlier that the playful activity of children is most evident in the absence of such motivating conditions, and Beach (1945) has reviewed evidence to show that animals are most likely to show playful activity when they are well fed, well watered, and in comfortable circumstances. Harlow, Harlow, and Meyer (1950) have found that monkeys learn to disassemble puzzles with no other motivation than the privilege of disassembling them. Similarly, Harlow (1950) found that two monkeys worked repeatedly at disassembling a six-device puzzle for ten continuous hours even though they were quite free of painful stimulation and homeostatic need. Moreover, as he notes, at the tenth hour of testing they were still "showing enthusiasm for their work."

In an important series of studies beginning in 1950, Berlyne (1960) found that comfortable and satiated rats will explore areas new to them if only given an opportunity, and that the more varied the objects in the region to be explored, the more persistent are the rats' explorations. In a similar vein, Montgomery (1952) has found that the spontaneous tendency for rats to go alternately to the opposite goal-boxes in a T- or Y-maze is no matter of fatigue for the most recently given re-

sponse, as Hull (1943) contended, but it is one of avoiding
the place which the animals have most recently experienced.
The choice of place is for the one of lesser familiarity (Montgomery, 1953), and rats learn merely in order to get an
opportunity to explore an unfamiliar area (Montgomery,
1955; Montgomery and Segall, 1955). In this same vein,
Butler (1953) has observed that monkeys will learn discriminations merely to obtain the privilege of peeking through a
window in the walls of their cages, or (Butler, 1958) of
listening to sounds from a tape recorder. All of these activities
appear to be most evident in the absence of painful stimulation, homeostatic need, and cues which have previously been
associated with such motivating stimuli. It is these findings
which call for a change in the traditionally dominant theoretical conception of motivation.

Some of the directions of change in belief show in the
modes of theoretical significance given to such evidence. One
of these ways is drive-naming. Thus, in recent years, we have
been hearing of a manipulatory drive, an exploratory drive, a
curiosity drive, etc. This form of theoretical recognition,
which is logically circular, appears to be revisiting Mc-
Dougall's (1908) theory of instincts.

A second mode of theoretical recognition is naming what
appears to be the telic significance of an activity. This is what
Ives Hendrick (1943) has done in conceiving of the delight
which children take in their new-found accomplishments as
evidence of an "urge to mastery." This is also what White
(1959) has done in his excellent review of such evidence by
attributing the various activities observed to "competence
motivation." Such terms of telic significance may be helpful
as classificatory and mnemonic devices, but they provide few
implications of antecedent-consequent relationships to be in-
vestigated.

A third mode of theoretical recognition has consisted in
postulating *spontaneous activity*. I have been guilty of this

(Hunt, 1960) and so also have Hebb (1949), Miller, Galanter, and Pribram (1960), and Taylor (1960). When, however, my good colleague, Lawrence I. O'Kelly, pointed out that the notion of spontaneous activity may be just as malevolently circular as drive- and instinct-naming, I could readily see the force of his argument. But I could also see that I had begun to discern at least the outlines of a mechanism of what I have termed "intrinsic motivation" or "motivation inherent in information processing and action" (Hunt, 1963a).

INTRINSIC MOTIVATION

The notion of the feedback loop provides a basis for "intrinsic motivation" and a new answer to the motivational question concerning what starts and what stops behavior. The start of behavior becomes a matter of incongruity between the input from a set of circumstances and some standard within the organism (Miller, Galanter, and Pribram, 1960); stopping becomes a matter of congruity. A variety of standards can be found within an organism's informational interaction with its circumstances. Perhaps the most primitive is the ongoing input of the moment. Whenever there is change in this standard, an organism exhibits what the Russians have termed the "orienting reflex" (see Berlyne, 1960; Razran, 1961). Other kinds deriving from experience are expectations, the self concept, aesthetic standards, and ideals. Another quite different category of standards resides within action, as something distinct from information processing (see Hunt, 1965) and appears to consist of ends and goals, or the "plans" of Miller, Galanter, and Pribram (1960).

The concept of incongruity also provides at least a tentative, hypothetical answer to the puzzling direction-hedonic question concerning what determines whether an organism will approach or withdraw from a source of input. Under conditions of changeless, homogeneous input, organisms will approach sources of incongruous or novel information (Nissen, 1930; Butler, 1953). In fact, when input remains change-less for too long, the situation becomes unbearable as demonstrated by the fact that McGill students would not remain in such a situation for longer than about three days even though they were paid $20 a day (Bexton, Heron, and Scott, 1954). On the other hand, withdrawal from a source of incongruous information also occurs when the discrepancy between the incoming information and that already in the storage is too great. This is apparently why an infant chimpanzee is frightened of its familiar and friendly caretaker seen in a Halloween mask (Hebb, 1946; Hebb and Riesen, 1943). The fact that incongruous information can elicit both an approach to its source and a withdrawal from its source may be puzzling until one notes that an optimum of incongruity is implied (see Hunt, 1943a). Inasmuch as organisms continually adapt to any given input, the need for an optimum implies an interest in what is novel but not too novel, what is incongruous but not too incongruous. The continual trend toward adaptation to existing input coupled with this interest in optimal incongruity provided a kind of explanation for the sort of "growth motivation" which Froebel (1826) postulated and which Dewey (1900) appears to have borrowed from Froebel. Relevant experiments in this area are few, Dember, Earl, and Paradise (1957) have found that when rats are given a choice between two figure-8 mazes differing in complexity, if they change their choice between two encounters with the maze, they regularly change from a choice of the less complex one to the more complex one. This optimum of incongruity gives to what I have elsewhere called "the problem of the match" (Hunt, 1961) a motivational meaning as well as an intellectual one. Interest in circumstances becomes a matter of a relationship between the new and the old wherein the new differs in proper degree from the old to provide the miss-match that elicits interest.

The basic structure of the motivational systems is essentially

preformed in the traditionally dominant theory. Piaget's
(1936) observations indicate, however, that there is an epigenesis in the structure of what I am calling "intrinsic motivation" as well as in the structure of intelligence and of reality
(see Hunt, 1963b). Three phases appear to characterize this
epigenesis, and whether these are stages in development in
general or stages merely in the infant's progressive relationships to any completely new set of circumstances (see Harvey,
Hunt, and Schroeder, 1961) is a moot question as of now.
During the first phase, the child is apparently motivated not
only by homeostatic need and painful stimulation, as O. C.
Irwin's (1930) classic studies have indicated, but also by
changes in ongoing input through the eyes and ears. These
changes in input elicit the "orienting reaction" of the Russian
investigators (see Berlyne, 1960; Razran, 1961), a reaction
consisting of attention and physiological evidences of arousal.
Such reactions appear to motivate the co-ordinating of the
ready-made systems described by Piaget (1936). The second
phase begins with the interest in the newly familiar that appears to come with repeated encounters with the same pattern of change in input. This interest is manifested by the
emergence of intentional efforts on the part of the child to
retain or to regain perceptual contact with repeatedly encountered patterns. It is apparently this interest in the newly familiar that motivates such autogenic activities as the repetitious
babbling commonly observed during the third and fourth
months, the persistent hand-watching that commonly begins
during the latter part of the fourth month, and the pseudo-
imitation of familiar patterns that have been remarked upon
by many observers of infant development. The third phase begins with the appearance of interest in novelty, commonly
about the end of the first year of life, or perhaps somewhat
earlier (see Hunt, 1961; 1963b). It shows in an interest in observing things like the trajectory of thrown objects and unfamiliar and unpracticed models, and of attempting new

means of achieving ends by a groping process. With this development of interest in novelty, the infant begins to acquire new vocal schemata, new gestures, and new interests in a rapidly widening variety of objects, persons, and places. With the development of interest in novelty comes the "growth motivation" illustrated by Dember, Earl, and Paradise (1957) and the "problem of the match" in its motivational guise.

APPLICATIONS OF SUCH THEORIZING FOR THE DEVELOPMENT OF AN ANTIDOTE FOR CULTURAL DEPRIVATION

It remains for me to examine some applications of the theoretical fabric that I have been weaving to the development of a pre-school enrichment program for the culturally deprived. First of all, cultural deprivation may be seen as a failure to provide an opportunity for infants and young children to have the experiences required for adequate development of those semi-autonomous central processes demanded for acquiring skill in the use of linguistic and mathematical symbols and for the analysis of causal relationships. The difference between the culturally deprived and the culturally privileged is, for children, analogous to the difference between cage-reared and pet-reared rats and dogs. At the present time, this notion of cultural deprivation or of social disadvantage is gross and undifferentiated, indeed. On the basis of the evidence and conceptions I have summarized, however, I believe the concept points in a very promising direction. It should be possible to arrange institutional settings where children now culturally deprived by the accident of the social class of their parents can be supplied with a set of encounters with circumstances which will provide an antidote for what they may have missed.

The important study of Skeels and Dye (1939), which met with such a derisive reception when it first appeared, is highly relevant in this context. It was based on a "clinical surprise." Two infants, one aged thirteen months with a Kuhlman IQ of 46 and the other aged sixteen months with an IQ of 35, after residence in the relatively homogeneous circumstances of a state orphanage, were committed to a state institution for the feeble-minded. Some six months later, a psychologist visiting the wards noted with surprise that these two infants had shown a remarkable degree of development. No longer did they show either the apathy or the locomotor retardation that had characterized them when they were committed. When they were again tested with the Kuhlman scale, moreover, the younger had an IQ of 77 and the older an IQ of 87—improvements of 31 and 52 points respectively, and within half a year. In the experiment which followed this clinical surprise, every one of a group of thirteen children showed a substantial gain in IQ upon being transferred from the orphanage to the institution for the feeble-minded. These gains ranged between 7 points and 58 points of IQ. On the other hand, twelve other youngsters, within the same age range but with a somewhat higher mean IQ, were left in the orphanage. When these children were retested after periods varying between twenty-one and forty-three months, all had shown a substantial decrease in IQ, ranging between 8 and 45 points of IQ, with five of these decreases exceeding 35 points.

In the last year and a half, Harold Skeels has been engaged in a follow-up study of the individuals involved in these two groups. With about three fourths of the individuals found, he has yet to find one of the group transferred from the orphanage to the institution for the feeble-minded who is not now maintaining himself effectively in society. Contrariwise, he had not yet found any one of the group remaining in the orphanage who is not now living with institutional support (personal communication). Although the question of the permanence of the effects of experiential deprivation during infancy is far from answered, such evidence as I have been able to find, and as I have summarized here, would indicate that if the experiential deprivation does not persist too long, it is reversible to a substantial degree. If this be true, the idea of enriching the cognitive fare in day-care centers and in nursery schools for the culturally deprived looks very promising.

The fact that cultural deprivation is such a global and undifferentiated conception at present invites at least speculative attempts to construe the nature of the deficit and to see wherein and when the infant of the poor and lower class parents is most likely to be experientially deprived.

One of the important features of lower class life in poverty is crowding. Many persons live in little space. Crowding, however, may be no handicap for a human infant during most of his first year of life. Although there is no certainty of this, it is conceivable that being a young infant among a large number of people living within a room may actually serve to provide such wide variations of visual and auditory inputs that it will facilitate development more than will the conditions typical of the culturally privileged during most of the first year.

During the second year, on the other hand, living under crowded conditions could well be highly hampering. As the infant begins to throw things and as he begins to develop his own methods of locomotion, he is likely to find himself getting in the way of adults already made ill-tempered by their own discomforts and by the fact that they are getting in each other's way. Such considerations are dramatized in Lewis' (1961) *The Children of Sánchez*, an anthropological study of life in poverty. In such a crowded atmosphere, the activities in which the child must indulge for the development of his own interests and skills must almost inevitably be sharply curbed.

Beginning in the third year, moreover, imitation of novel patterns should presumably be well established, and should supply a mechanism for learning vocal language. The variety of linguistic patterns available for imitation in the models provided by lower class adults is both highly limited and wrong for the standards of later schooling. Furthermore, when the infant has developed a number of pseudowords and has achieved the "learning set" that "things have names" and begins asking "what's that?", he is all too unlikely to get answers. Or, the answers he gets are all too likely to be so punishing that they inhibit such questioning. The fact that his parents are preoccupied with the problems associated with their poverty and their crowded living conditions leaves them with little capacity to be concerned with what they conceive to be the senseless questions of a prattling infant. With things to play with and room to play in highly limited, the circumstances of the crowded lower class offer little opportunity for the kinds of environmental encounters required to keep a two-year-old youngster developing at all, and certainly not at an optimal rate and not in the direction demanded for adaptation in a highly technological culture.

If this armchair analysis has any validity, it suggests that the infant developing in the crowded circumstances of lower class poverty may develop well through the first year; begin to show retardation during the second year; and show even more retardation during the third, fourth, and fifth years. Presumably, that retardation which occurs during the second year, and even that during the third year, can probably be reversed to a considerable degree by supplying proper circumstances in either a nursery school or a day-care center for children of four and five—but I suspect it would be preferable to start with children at three years of age. The analysis made here, which is based largely upon what I have learned from Piaget (1936) and from my own observations of development during the preschool years, could be tested. Dr. Ina Uzgiris and I are attempting to develop a way of using the sensorimotor and early symbolic schemata which Piaget has described for the first two, and hopefully three, years of the child's life, to provide a method of assessing intellectual and motivational development. If our effort is successful, it should provide a tool with which to determine when and how the conditions of development within the crowded circumstances of poverty begin to result in retardation and/or apathy.

Our traditional emphasis in education upon arithmetic and language skills can well lead us astray in the attempt to develop a program of pre-school enrichment. If Piaget's (1945) observations are correct, spoken language—that is to say the motor side of the language skill—comes only after images, or the central processes representing objects and events, have been developed out of repeated encounters with those objects and events. The fact that chimpanzees show clearly the capacity to dissemble their own purposes even though they lack language (Hebb and Thompson, 1954) lends support from phylogenetic comparisons to this notion of Piaget's. Omar K. Moore has been teaching pre-school children to read with the aid of an electric typewriter hooked up to an electronic system of storing and retrieving information. The fact that children, once they have learned to recognize letters by pressing the proper keys of a typewriter, are then enabled to discover spontaneously that they can draw these letters with chalk on a blackboard, lends further support to the image-primacy thesis. Moreover, Moore has observed that the muscular control of such four-year-olds as have presumably acquired solid imagery of the letters in the course of their experience with those letters at the electric typewriter corresponds to that typical of seven- or eight-year-olds (personal communication).

What appears to be important for a pre-school enrichment program is an opportunity to encounter circumstances which will foster the development of these semiautonomous central processes that can serve as imagery representative of objects and events and which can become the referents for the spoken symbols required in the phonemic combinations of spoken or written language. Moore's results also suggest to me that these semiautonomous central processes, if adequately developed, can serve as the basis for motor control. Such considerations suggest that a proper pre-school enrichment program should provide children with an opportunity to encounter a wide variety of objects and circumstances. They suggest that the children should also have an opportunity to imitate a wide variety of models of action and of motor language. The danger of attempting to prescribe materials and models at this stage of knowledge, however, is that the prescriptions may well fail to provide a proper match with what the child already has in his storage. The fact that most teachers have their expectations based on experience with culturally privileged children makes this problem of the match especially dangerous and vexing in work with the culturally deprived.

In view of the dangers of attempting prescriptions of enrichments for pre-school children, it may be well to re-examine the educational contributions of Maria Montessori. Until recently, I could have identified Maria Montessori only by saying that she had developed some kind of kindergarten and was an educational faddist who had made quite a splash about the turn of the century. I was introduced to her work by Dr. Jan Smedslund, a Norwegian psychologist, who remarked to me, during a conference at the University of Colorado, that Maria Montessori had provided a practical answer to what I have called "the problem of the match" (Hunt, 1961).

When I examined the library for materials on Maria Montessori, I discovered that the novelist, Dorothy Canfield Fisher, had spent the winter of 1910–1911 at the Casa de Bambini in Rome and that she had returned to write a book on Montessori's work. This book, entitled *A Montessori Mother* (1912), may still be the best initial introduction to Montessori's work. Books by E. M. Standing (1957) and Nancy Rambusch (1962) have brought the record up to date, and the book by Rambusch contains a bibliography of the materials in the English language concerning Montessori's work assembled by Gilbert E. Donahue.

Montessori's contribution is especially interesting to me because she based her methods of teaching upon the spontaneous interest of children in learning, that is, upon what I am calling "intrinsic motivation." Moreover, she put great stress upon teachers observing the children under their care to discover what kinds of things foster their individual interests and growth. Furthermore, she put great stress on the training of what she called sensory processes, but what we might more appropriately call information processes today. The fact that she placed strong emphasis upon the training of sensory processes may well be one of the major reasons why her work dropped out of the mainstream of educational thought and practice in America before World War I. This emphasis was too dissonant with the dominant American emphasis in learning upon the motor response, rather than upon the sensory input or information processes. It was Montessori's concern to observe carefully what interested a child that led her to discover a wide variety of materials in which she found children showing strong spontaneous interest.

Secondly, Montessori broke the lock step in the education of young children. Her schools made no effort to keep all the children doing the same thing at the same time. Rather, each child was free to examine and to work with whatever happened to interest him. This meant that he was free to persist in a given concern as long as he cared to, and also free to change from one concern to another whenever a change appeared appropriate to him. In this connection, one of the very interesting observations made by Dorothy Canfield Fisher concerns the prolonged duration that children remain interested in given activities under such circumstances. Whereas the lore about pre-schoolers holds that the nature of the activity in a nursery school must be changed every ten or fifteen minutes, Mrs. Fisher described children typically remaining engrossed in such activities as the buttoning and unbuttoning of a row of buttons for two or more hours at a time.

Thirdly, Montessori's method consisted in having children aged from three to six years old together. As I see it, from taking into account the epigenesis of intellectual development, such a scheme has the advantage of providing the younger children with a wide variety of models for imitation. Moreover, it supplies the older children with an opportunity to help and teach the younger. Helping and teaching contain many of their own rewards.

Perhaps the chief advantage of Montessori's method lies in the fact that it gives the individual child an opportunity to find the circumstances which match his own particular interests and stage of development. This carries with it the corollary advantage of making learning fun.

There may be yet another advantage, one in which those financing pre-school enrichment will be heartily concerned. Montessori's first teacher was a teenage girl, the daughter of the superintendent of the apartment house in the slums of Rome where the first of the Case dei Bambini was established in 1907. In that school this one young woman successfully taught, or should we say, set the stage for the learning of, between fifty and sixty children ranging in age from three to six years old. I say "successfully" because, as Dorothy Canfield Fisher (1912) reports, a substantial proportion of these children learned to read by the time they were five years old. Moreover, they had learned it spontaneously through their own intrinsic motivation, and they appeared to enjoy the process. This observation hints that Montessori's contribution may also contain suggestions of importance economically.

SUMMARY

I began by saying that it was very exciting for me to encounter people, who are generally considered sensible, to be in the process of planning to utilize pre-school experience as an antidote for the effects of cultural deprivation. I have tried to summarize the basis in psychological theory and in the evidence from psychological research for such a use of pre-school enrichment. I have tried to summarize the evidence showing: *notable*
(1) that the belief in fixed intelligence is no longer tenable;
(2) that development is far from completely predetermined;

(3) that what goes on between the ears is much less like the static switchboard of the telephone than it is like the active information processes programmed into electronic computers to enable them to solve problems; (4) that experience is the programmer of the human brain-computer, and thus Freud was correct about the importance of the experience which comes before the advent of language; (5) that, nonetheless, Freud was wrong about the nature of the experience which is important, since an opportunity to see and hear a variety of things appears to be more important than the fate of instinctual needs and impulses; and, finally, (6) that learning need not be motivated by painful stimulation, homeostatic need, or the acquired drives based upon these, for there is a kind of intrinsic motivation which is inherent in information processing and action.

In applying these various lines of evidence and these various changes in conception, I have viewed the effects of cultural deprivation as analogous to the experimentally found effects of experiential deprivation in infancy. I have pointed out the importance and the dangers of deriving from "the problem of the match" in attempting to prescribe from existing knowledge a program of circumstantial encounters for the purpose of enriching the experience of culturally deprived preschool children. In this connection, I have suggested that we re-examine the work of Maria Montessori for suggestions about how to proceed. For she successfully based her teaching method on the spontaneous interest of children in learning, and answered the problem of the match with careful observation of what interests children and by giving them individual freedom to choose which of the various circumstances made available they would encounter at any given time.

BIBLIOGRAPHY

BEACH, F. A., "Current Concepts of Play in Animals," *American Naturalist*, 79:523–541, 1945.

BERLYNE, D. E., *Conflict, Arousal, and Curiosity*. New York: McGraw-Hill, 1960.

BEXTON, W. H., W. HERON, and T. H. SCOTT, "Effects of Decreased Variation in the Sensory Environment," *Canadian Journal of Psychology*, 8:70–76, 1954.

BORING, E. G., *A History of Experimental Psychology*. New York: Century, 1929.

BRATTGÅRD, S. O., The Importance of Adequate Stimulation for the Chemical Composition of Retinal Ganglion Cells during Early Postnatal Development, *Acta radiologica*, Supplement 96, Stockholm, 1952.

BÜHLER, K., "Displeasure and Pleasure in Relation to Activity." In M. L. Reymert (ed.), *Feelings and Emotions: The Wittenberg Symposium*. Worcester, Massachusetts: Clark University Press, 1928, ch. 14.

BUTLER, R. A., "Discrimination Learning by Rhesus Monkeys to Visual Exploration Motivation." *Journal of Comparative Physiological Psychology*, 46:95–98, 1953.

———— "The Differential Effect of Visual and Auditory Incentives on the Performance of Monkeys," *American Journal of Psychology*, 71:591–593, 1958

CARMICHAEL, L., "The Development of Behavior in Vertebrates Experimentally Removed from the Influence of External Stimulation," *Psychological Review*, 33:51–58, 1926.

———— "A Further Study of the Development of Behavior in Vertebrates Experimentally Removed from the Influence of External Stimulation," *Psychological Review*, 34:34–47, 1927.

———— "A Further Study of the Development of Behavior . . . ," *Psychological Review*, 35:253–260, 1928.

CATTELL, J. McK., "Mental Tests and Measurements." *Mind*, 15:373–381, 1890.

COGHILL, G. E., *Anatomy and the Problem of Behaviour*. Cambridge: Cambridge University Press, 1929.

CRUZE, W. W., "Maturation and Learning in Chicks," *Journal of Comparative Psychology*, 19:371–409, 1935.

———— "Maturation and Learning Ability," *Psychological Monographs*, 50, No. 5, 1938.

DARWIN, CHARLES, *Origin of Species*. London: Murray, 1859.

———— *The Expressions of the Emotions in Man and Animals*. New York: Appleton, 1873 (originally published: London: Murray, 1872).

DASHIELL, J. F., *Fundamentals of Objective Psychology*. New York: Houghton Mifflin, 1928.

DEMBER, W. N., R. W. EARL, and N. PARADISE, "Response by Rats to Differential Stimulus Complexity," *Journal of Comparative Physiological Psychology*, 50:514–518, 1957.

DENENBERG, V. H., "The Effects of Early Experience." In E. S. E. Hafez (ed.), *The Behaviour of Domestic Animals*. London: Baillière, Tindall & Cox, 1962.

DENNIS, W., "Causes of Retardation among Institutional Children," *Journal of Genetic Psychology*, 96:47–59, 1960.

DENNIS, W., and MARSENA G. DENNIS, "The Effect of Restricted Practice upon the Reaching, Sitting and Standing of Two Infants," *Journal of Genetic Psychology*, 47:21–29, 1935.

———— "Infant Development under Conditions of Restricted Practice and Minimum Social Stimulation: A Preliminary Report," *Journal of Genetic Psychology*, 53:151–156, 1938.

———— "The Effect of Cradling Practice upon the Onset of Walking in Hopi Children," *Journal of Genetic Psychology*, 56:77–86, 1940.

———— "Infant Development under Conditions of Restricted Practice and Minimum Social Stimulation," *Genetic Psychology Monographs*, 23:149–155, 1941.

DEWEY, JOHN, *The School and Society*. Chicago: University of Chicago Press, Phoenix Books, P3, 1960. (First published 1900.)

———— The Child and the Curriculum. Chicago: University of Chicago Press, Phoenix Books, P3, 1960. (First published 1902.)

FARBER, I. E., "Response Fixation under Anxiety and Non-anxiety Conditions," *Journal of Experimental Psychology*, 38:111–131, 1948.

FENICHEL, O., *The Psychoanalytic Theory of Neurosis*. New York: Norton, 1945.

FISHER, DOROTHY CANFIELD, *A Montessori Mother*. New York: Holt, 1912.

FISKE, D. W., and S. R. MADDI, *Functions of Varied Experience*. Homewood, Illinois: Dorsey Press, 1961.

FREEDMAN, A., "Drive Conditioning in Water Deprivation." Unpublished Ph.D. dissertation, University of Illinois, 1957.

FREEMAN, G. L., *Introduction to Physiological Psychology*. New York: Ronald, 1934.

FREUD, SIGMUND, "The Interpretation of Dreams." In A. A. Brill (tr. & ed.), *The Basic Writings of Sigmund Freud*. New York: Modern Library, 1938. (*The Interpretation of Dreams* originally published 1900.)

———— "The Psychopathology of Everyday Life." In A. A. Brill (tr. & ed.), *The Basic Writings of Sigmund Freud*. New York: Modern Library, 1938 (*Three Contributions to the Theory of Sex* originally published 1905.)

———— "Instincts and Their Vicissitudes," *Collected Papers*, 4:60–83. London: Hogarth, 1927. (*Instincts and Their Vicissitudes* originally published 1915.)

———— *The Problem of Anxiety* (H. A. Bunker, tr.). New York: Norton, 1936. (*Hemmung, Symptom, und Angst* originally published 1926.)

FROEBEL, F., *The Education of Man* (W. N. Hailmann, tr.). New York: Appleton, 1896. (*Die Menschenerziehung* originally published 1826.)

GALTON, F., *Hereditary Genius: An Inquiry into Its Laws and Consequences*. London: Macmillan, 1869.

GAURON, E. F., and W. C. BECKER, "The Effects of Early Sensory Deprivation on Adult Rat Behavior under Competition Stress: An Attempt at Replication of a Study by Alexander Wolf," *Journal of Comparative Physiological Psychology*, 52: 689–693, 1959.

GESELL, ARNOLD, *The Embryology of Human Behavior: The Beginnings of the Human Mind.* New York: Harper, 1945.

—— "The Ontogenesis of Infant Behavior." In L. Carmichael (ed.), *Manual of Child Psychology.* New York: Wiley, 1954, ch. 6.

GESELL, A., and HELEN THOMPSON, Learning and Growth in Identical Twin Infants. *Genetic Psychology Monographs,* 6:1–124, 1929.

GODDARD, H. H., *The Kallikak Family: A Study in the Heredity of Feeble-mindedness.* New York: Macmillan, 1912.

GOLDMAN, JACQUELIN R., "The Effects of Handling and Shocking in Infancy upon Adult Behavior in the Albino Rat," *Journal of Genetic Psychology,* 102, 1964.

GOODENOUGH, FLORENCE, "A Critique of Experiments on Raising the I.Q." *Educational Method,* 19:73–79, 1939.

GUTHRIE, E. R., *The Psychology of Human Conflict: The Clash of Motives within the Individual.* New York: Harper, 1938.

HALL, C. S., "Emotional Behavior in the Rat: I. Defecation and Urination as Measures of Individual Differences in Emotionality," *Journal of Comparative Psychology,* 18:385–403, 1934.

HALL, M., *New Mémoire on the Nervous System.* London: Proceedings of the Royal Academy, 1843.

HARLOW, H. F., "Learning and Satiation of Response in Intrinsically Motivated Complex Puzzle Performance by Monkeys," *Journal of Comparative Physiological Psychology,* 43:289–294, 1950.

—— "The Nature of Love," *American Psychologist,* 13:673–685, 1958.

HARLOW, H. F., M. K. HARLOW, and D. R. MEYER, "Learning Motivated by a Manipulation Drive," *Journal of Experimental Psychology,* 40:228–234, 1950.

HARVEY, O. J., D. E. HUNT, and H. M. SCHROEDER, *Conceptual Systems and Personality Organization.* New York: Wiley, 1961.

HEBB, D. O., "On the Nature of Fear," *Psychological Review,* 53:259–276, 1946.

—— "The Effects of Early Experience on Problem-solving at Maturity," *American Psychologist,* 2:306–307, 1947.

—— *The Organization of Behavior.* New York: Wiley, 1949.

HEBB, D. O., and A. H. RIESEN, "The Genesis of Irrational Fears," *Canadian Psychological Association Bulletin,* 3:49–50, 1943.

HEBB, D. O., and W. R. THOMPSON, "The Social Significance of Animal Studies." In G. Lindzey (ed.), *Handbook of Social Psychology.* Cambridge, Massachusetts: Addison-Wesley, 1954, ch. 15.

HEBB, D. O., and K. WILLIAMS, "A Method of Rating Animal Intelligence," *Journal of Genetic Psychology,* 34:59–65, 1946.

HENDRICK, I., "The Discussion of the 'Instinct to Master,'" *Psychoanalytic Quarterly,* 12:561–565, 1943.

HERNANDEZ-PEON, R., H. SCHERRER, and M. JOUVET, "Modification of Electric Activity in Cochlear Nucleus during 'Attention' in Unanesthetized Cats," *Science,* 123:331–332, 1956.

HILGARD, JOSEPHINE R., "Learning and Maturation in Pre-School Children," *Journal of Genetic Psychology,* 41:36–56, 1932.

HOLMES, FRANCES, B. "An Experimental Study of Children's Fears." In A. T. Jersild and Frances B. Holmes (eds.), *Children's Fears.* New York: Columbia University, Teachers College (*Child Development Monograph,* 20), 1935.

HOLT, E. B., *Animal Drive and the Learning Process.* New York: Holt, 1931.

HULL, C. L., "Goal Attraction and Directing Ideas Conceived as Habit Phenomena," *Psychological Review,* 38:487–506, 1931.

—— *Principles of Behavior.* New York: Appleton-Century, 1943.

HUNT, J. McV., "The Effects of Infant Feeding-Frustration upon Adult Hoarding in the Albino Rat," *Journal of Abnormal and Social Psychology,* 36:338–360, 1941.

—— "Experimental Psychoanalysis." In P. L. Harriman (ed.), *Encyclopedia of Psychology.* New York: Philosophical Library, 1945.

————— "Psychosexual Development: The Infant Disciplines." Unpublished manuscript of a chapter written for *Behavioral Science and Child Rearing*, 1956.

————— "Experience and the Development of Motivation: Some Reinterpretations," *Child Development*, 31:489–504, 1960.

————— *Intelligence and Experience.* New York: Ronald, 1961.

————— "Motivation Inherent in Information Processing and Action." In O. J. Harvey (ed.), *Cognitive Factors in Motivation and Social Organization.* New York: Ronald, 1963 (a).

————— "Piaget's Observations as a Source of Hypotheses Concerning Motivation," *Merrill-Palmer Quarterly of Behavior and Development*, 9:263–275, 1963 (b).

————— "Intrinsic Motivation and Its Role in Development," *Nebraska Symposium on Motivation*, 13:198–274, 1965.

HUNT, J. McV., and ZELLA LURIA, "Investigations of the Effects of Early Experience in Subhuman Animals." Unpublished manuscript of a chapter written for *Behavioral Science and Child Rearing*, 1956.

HUNTER, W. S., "The Delayed Reaction in Animals and Children." *Behavior Monographs*, 2, No. 1:1–85, 1912.

————— "The Temporal Maze and Kinaesthetic Sensory Processes in the White Rat," *Psychobiology*, 2:339–351, 1918.

HYDÉN, H., "Biochemical Changes in Glial Cells and Nerve Cells at Varying Activity." In F. Brücke (ed.), *Proceedings of the Fourth International Congress of Biochemistry*, III, *Biochemistry of the Central Nervous System*. London: Pergamon, 1959.

————— "The Neuron." In J. Brachet and A. E. Mirsky (eds.), *The Cell: Biochemistry, Physiology, Morphology*, IV. *Specialized Cells*. New York: Academic Press, pp. 215–323, 1960.

IRWIN, O. C., "The Amount and Nature of Activities of Newborn Infants under Constant External Stimulating Conditions during the First 10 Days of Life," *Genetic Psychology Monographs*, 8:192, 1930.

KÖHLER, W., *The Mentality of Apes.* New York: Harcourt, Brace, 1925.

LAMARCK, J. CHEVALIER DE, *Zoological Philosophy (Philosophie Zoologique,* tr. by H. Elliot). London: Macmillan, 1914. Originally published 1809.

LEVINE, S., J. A. CHEVALIER, and S. J. KORCHIN, The Effects of Early Shock and Handling on Later Avoidance Learning. *Personnel Journal,* 24:475–493, 1956.

LEWIS, OSCAR, *The Children of Sánchez.* New York: Random House, 1961.

LIBERMAN, R., "Retinal Cholinesterase and Glycolysis in Rats Raised in Darkness," *Science,* 135:372–373, 1962.

McDOUGALL, W., *An Introduction to Social Psychology.* Boston: Luce, 1908.

McGRAW, MYRTLE B., *Growth: A Study of Johnny and Jimmy.* New York: Appleton-Century, 1935.

MELTON, A. W., "Learning." In W. S. Munroe (ed.), *Encyclopedia of Educational Research.* New York: Macmillan, 1941.

MILLER, G. A., E. H. GALANTER, and K. H. PRIBRAM, *Plans and the Structure of Behavior.* New York: Holt, 1960.

MILLER, N. E., and J. DOLLARD, *Social Learning and Imitation.* New Haven: Yale University Press, 1941.

MONTGOMERY, K. C., "A Test of Two Explanations of Spontaneous Alternation," *Journal of Comparative Physiological Psychology,* 45:287–293, 1952.

——— "Exploratory Behavior as a Function of 'Similarity' of Stimulus Situations," *Journal of Comparative Physiological Psychology,* 46:129–133, 1953.

——— "The Relation between Fear Induced by Novel Stimulation and Exploratory Behavior." *Journal of Comparative Physiological Psychology,* 48:254–260, 1955.

MONTGOMERY, K. C., and M. SEGALL, "Discrimination Learning Based upon the Exploratory Drive," *Journal of Comparative Physiological Psychology,* 48:225–228, 1955.

MORGAN, C. LLOYD, *An Introduction to Comparative Psychology* (2d ed.). London: Scott, 1909. Originally published, 1894.

MOWRER, O. H., *Learning Theory and Behavior.* New York: Wiley, 1960.

NEWELL, A., J. C. SHAW, and H. A. SIMON, "Elements of a Theory of Human Problem Solving," *Psychological Review,* 65: 151–166, 1958.

NISSEN, H. W., "A Study of Exploratory Behavior in the White Rat by means of the Obstruction Method," *Journal of Genetic Psychology,* 37:361–376, 1930.

ORLANSKY, H., "Infant Care and Personality," *Psychological Bulletin,* 46:1–48, 1949.

OSGOOD, C. E., "The Nature and Measurement of Meaning," *Psychological Bulletin,* 49:192–237, 1952.

PIAGET, J., *The Origins of Intelligence in Children* (Margaret Cook, tr.). New York: International Universities Press, 1952. Originally published 1936.

—— *Play, Dreams, and Imitation in Childhood* (C. Gattegno and F. M. Hodgson, tr.). New York: Norton, 1951. Originally published as *La formation du symbole chez l'enfant,* 1945.

—— *The Psychology of Intelligence* (M. Piercy and D. E. Berlyne, trs.). London: Routledge & Kegan Paul, 1947.

PRIBRAM, K. H., A Review of Theory in Physiological Psychology. *Annual Review Psychology,* 11:1–40, 1960.

PRUETTE, LORINE, *G. Stanley Hall: A Biography of a Mind.* New York: Appleton, 1926.

RAMBUSCH, NANCY M., *Learning How to Learn: An American Approach to Montessori.* Baltimore: Helicon Press, 1962.

RASCH, E., H. SWIFT, A. H. RIESEN, and K. L. CHOW, "Altered Structure and Composition of Retinal Cells in Dark-reared Mammals," *Experimental Cell Research,* 25:348–363, 1961.

RAZRAN, G., "The Observable Unconscious and the Inferable Conscious in Current Soviet Psychophysiology: Interoceptive Conditioning, Semantic Conditioning, and the Orienting Reflex." *Psychological Review,* 68:81–147, 1961.

RIESEN, A. H., "Plasticity of Behavior: Psychological Aspects." In H. F. Harlow and C. N. Woolsey (eds.), *Biological and Biochemical Bases of Behavior.* Madison: University of Wisconsin Press, 1958, pp. 425–450.

ROMANES, G. J., *Animal Intelligence.* New York: Appleton, 1883.

—— *Mental Evolution in Animals.* New York: Appleton, 1884.

ROSE, J. E., and C. N. WOOLSEY, "The Relations of Thalamic Connections, Cellular Structure, and Evocable Electrical Activity in the Auditory Region of the Cat." *Journal of Comparative Neurology,* 91:441–466, 1949.

ROUSSEAU, J. J., *Emile* (Barbara Foxley, tr.). New York: Everyman's Library, 1916. Originally published 1762.

SALAMA, A. A., and J. McV. HUNT, "Fixation in the Rat as a Function of Infantile Shocking, Handling, and Gentling," *Journal of Genetic Psychology,* 100, 1964.

SCHNEIRLA, T. C., "An Evolutionary and Developmental Theory of Biphasic Processes Underlying Approach and Withdrawal." In M. R. Jones (ed.), *Nebraska Symposium on Motivation.* Lincoln: University of Nebraska Press, 1959, pp. 1–43.

SHERRINGTON, C. S., *The Integrative Action of the Nervous System.* New York: Scribner, 1906.

SIMPSON, B. R., The Wandering IQ. *Journal of Psychology,* 7:351–367, 1939.

SKEELS, H. M., and H. B. DYE, "A Study of the Effects of Differential Stimulation on Mentally Retarded Children." *Proceedings of the American Association on Mental Deficiency,* 44:114–136, 1939.

SPITZ, R. A., "The Smiling Response: A Contribution to the Ontogenesis of Social Relations," *Genetic Psychology Monographs,* 34:67–125, 1946.

STANDING, E. M., *Maria Montessori: Her Life and Work.* Fresno, California: Academy Library Guild, 1957.

STODDARD, G. D., and BETH L. WELLMAN, "Environment and the IQ," *National Society for the Study of Education Yearbook,* 39 (I), 405–442, 1940.

TAYLOR, D. W., "Toward an Information Processing Theory of Motivation." In M. R. Jones (ed.), *Nebraska Symposium on Motivation.* Lincoln: University of Nebraska Press, 1960, pp. 51–79.

THOMPSON, W. R., and W. HERON, "The Effects of Restricting Early Experience on the Problem-solving Capacity of Dogs," *Canadian Journal of Psychology,* 8:17–31, 1954.

THORNDIKE, E. L., *Educational Psychology*. Vol. II, *The Psychology of Learning*. New York: Columbia University Press, 1913.

THORNDIKE, E. L., and R. S. WOODWORTH, "The Influence of Improvement in One Mental Function upon the Efficiency of other Functions," *Psychological Review*, 8:247–261, 384–395, 553–564, 1901.

WALKER, A. E., and T. A. WEAVER, JR., "Ocular Movements from the Occipital Lobe in the Monkey," *Journal of Neurophysiology*, 3:353–357, 1940.

WATSON, J. B., *Psychology from the Standpoint of a Behaviorist*. Philadelphia: Lippincott, 1919.

——— *The Psychological Care of the Infant and Child*. New York: Norton, 1928.

WATSON, J. B., and R. RAYNER, *"Conditioned Emotional Reactions," Journal of Experimental Psychology*, 3:1–14, 1920.

WEISKRANTZ, L., "Sensory Deprivation and the Cat's Optic Nervous System," *Nature*, 181, (3), 47–1050, 1958.

WHITE, R. W., "Motivation Reconsidered: The Concept of Competence," *Psychological Review*, 66:297–333, 1959.

WIENER, NORBERT, *Cybernetics*. New York: Wiley, 1948.

WOLF, A., "The Dynamics of the Selective Inhibition of Specific Functions in Neuroses." *Psychosomatic Medicine*, 5:27–38, 1943.

WOODWORTH, R. S., "Heredity and Environment: A Critical Study of Recently Published Material on Twins and Foster Children," *Social Science Research Council Bulletin*, No. 47, 1941.

4. Facilitating Development in the Pre-School Child: Social and Psychological Perspectives

Martin Deutsch[1]

Massive evidence makes it clear that a child's social experience is a very influential factor in his development; yet it is also obvious that the relationship between experience and development is an extremely complex one.

In a sense, our current social dilemma has the usual contradictions that every period feels are unique to its particular time. Historically, the present era may or may not have more contradictions than other periods. But the rapid development of automated, highly skilled, labor-reducing techniques does have revolutionary consequences for man's relationship to the social order, to work and leisure, and to intellectual activity. Further, the level of our technology, particularly in the field of communication, creates conditions in which these new techniques are rapidly disseminated. Thus, the time within which institutional and structural adjustments can take place is greatly reduced. This necessitates the deliberate and planned manipulation of social conditions in order to avoid, or at least attenuate, the sometimes invidious consequences of rapid change.

[1] This article was prepared for the Arden House Conference on Pre-School Enrichment of Socially Disadvantaged Children (December 1962) and appeared in the *Merrill-Palmer Quarterly of Behavior and Development,* Volume 10, Number 3, July 1964.

In a society of abundance, there is an amazingly large segment of our population living in a subsociety of social, economic, and educational impoverishment. The estimates range from 20 to 40 per cent of our population, depending on criteria. The problems associated with marginal employment and crowded, dehumanizing living conditions are, of course, characteristic of the lives of most of the peoples of the world. But here in this country we have the facilities, the productive capacity, and at least some of the knowledge required consciously to reorient social development. A necessary focus for such orientation should be the child, so that he can develop the requisite basic skills for the new technology and changing social institutions.

A thesis presented in this article is that the behavioral scientist and the educator can facilitate the evolution of the educational institution so that it will be capable of preparing all children for optimal social participation, as the racial, social class, and sex gatekeepers become inoperative. The contemporary problems of education are to some extent a reflection of current technological, racial, and urban conflicts inherent in accelerated social change. At the same time, the human sciences (though beset by similar problems) could become major instrumentalities for the resolution of social conflict, since they are among the few systems oriented toward change. For example, the intervention concepts in social psychology and psychiatry are relatively quite new. These disciplines can thus be seen as possible agents for the construction of blueprints to harmonize human needs with cultural transformations.

In general, the human sciences are moving from social and individual diagnosis to remedial therapies. Those sciences are now, in some of the more advanced thinking, concerned with primary prevention, ranging from mental illness and juvenile delinquency to disabilities in learning and socialization. To speculate on a possible avenue of future development, it might be that from this stage an orientation will develop toward assisting the individual to potentiate his intrinsic capacities for productive living and full individual realization.

This is by no means meant to minimize the importance of activities in other disciplines; rather, it is an attempt to specify the potential role and contribution of the human sciences. It must also be remarked that the knowledge available in the combined human sciences is still quite limited, and that too frequently formulas have been presented which are insufficiently related to scientific knowledge.

While to a major degree the behavioral sciences and education have run parallel courses, they have insufficiently interacted with and enriched each other. What better place is there to investigate meaningfully the development of learning processes—or of attitudes or of mental health—than in longitudinal studies in the context of the school, from the nursery school through college? It is always surprising to us how many educators are not aware of the exciting investigations of socialization, learning, and cognitive processes in the field of child development. On the other hand, too many social scientists look upon education and work in the educational field as "applied," "atheoretical," and somehow unrelated to the growth of a child into an adult. Just as medicine is the application of physiology, biochemistry, and similar sciences to human problems, so too could education be the application of the human sciences. As medicine discovers principles and laws that are continually being circulated back to its basic sciences, so could education not only evaluate and validate the principles which it derives from the human sciences, but also lead toward the genesis of methods of influencing and accelerating individual growth.

In order to achieve such integration, a crucial historical difference between education and psychiatry, sociology and psychology must be recognized. While the latter have the impetus coming from both their newness and their response to challenge, education has the disadvantage of a long and encumbering history. In a sense, the institution of education—the school—*is* the status quo. Often it must operate through politically oriented bureaucracies that continually inhibit its potential for change and for developing strategies to meet social crises such as those inherent in the new urban America. These bureaucracies are often so large that introduction of meaningful change, even when agreed on by the higher echelons, is limited by the clogging of communication channels with paper, red tape, and assorted other artifacts, and by the constraints under which the average classroom teacher operates.

Somehow, this great gap in the educational hierarchy, separating the educator and his concept from the classroom teacher with her idea, creates a discontinuity that results in much wasted energy and distortion of effort. A clear educational philosophy can come best from educators who are free enough from bureaucracy to communicate with the classroom teacher as a full professional, and to attenuate the burden of the past while setting up new relationships with the human sciences. Inherent in this approach is the necessity for effective co-operation between educators and behavioral scientists, so as to incorporate the growing knowledge of the sociopsychological development of the child into educational procedures in the interests of facilitating realization of his greatest intellectual and social potential.

PREVENTING LEARNING DISABILITIES AND FACILITATING INTELLECTUAL GROWTH

The children most in need of help are from the economically and socially marginal and quasi-marginal segments of the community. These groups are the ones most caught in the technological and social changes; in many of our metropolitan areas they are becoming the majority of the center city population. It is in these groups that we find the highest proportion of unemployment, welfare support, and broken families. And it is in their children that we see the highest proportion of

~~learning disabilities and school dropouts~~. While in the past it was possible to absorb most of such youth in unskilled, low-paying jobs, now the current adult generation is increasingly being replaced in such jobs by machines. With the number of unskilled and semiskilled jobs decreasing, in order to find any place in the job market youth must now learn more complex functions, for which a successful educational experience is a prerequisite. This is a central problem for the total community, and a challenge for education. How it is met has wide ramifications for other underdeveloped areas outside our large cities and national boundaries.

There are various avenues of approach to the problem of both preventing learning disabilities and facilitating intellectual growth.

In recent years, ~~there have been major curriculum renovations, enrichment programs, new systems for teaching mathematics and the sciences, programmed courses and teaching machines,~~ as well as a multiplicity of ~~new methods for teaching reading~~. However, in the disadvantaged, underdeveloped areas of our communities, where there is the large proportion of underachievers, these new methods are probably least applicable, being most often based on an assumption that the child has reached a particular level in skills which underlie them. As will be pointed out later, for the disadvantaged child this is an unwarranted assumption. For the most part, it is a correct assumption for the middle-class child; but here there are other problems. Too often, new methods are seen mainly as more effective techniques to help the child get into college and achieve occupation status goals, and the aim of education along with its innovations becomes narrowly pragmatic. This is not to say that new methods should not be devised and attempted, but rather, that they might be seen neither as solutions to underachievement nor as substitutions for the development and encouragement of intrinsic motivation toward intellectual mastery and scholastic achievement.

An approach that combines the preventive with the facilitating—and which would establish a basis for the absorption of new methods—is that of planned intervention at the earlier periods of development of the various components of the intellectual spectrum. Evidence which is accumulating points more and more to the influence of background variables on the patterns of language and cognitive development of the child, and a subsequent diffusion of the effects of such patterns into all areas of the child's academic and psychological performance. Deprived backgrounds thus lead to the inadequacy of such patterns. What is proposed is that experiential inadequacies in the social background can be compensated for by a planned enrichment, channeled through improved schools.

URBAN SLUM LIFE AND EDUCATIONAL ACHIEVEMENT

Reference has been made to the constellation of factors in lower class life which are associated with a limited range of experiential variability available to the child. Of course, there are probably differing clusters of economic, social, and family factors associated with greater or lesser retardation. But the fact remains that lower social class status apparently predisposes to scholastic retardation, even though not all children are equally affected. Therefore, before discussing learning processes in the school it might be helpful to delineate some of the major features of urban slum life.

Geographically, there are crowded and dilapidated tenements quite at variance with the TV image of how people live. If the people are Negro, Puerto Rican, or Mexican-American, or poor mountain white, life is in a more or less segregated community. There are likely to be extremely crowded apartments, high rates of unemployment, chronic economic insecurity, a disproportionate number of broken families, and (particularly in the case of the Negro) continual exposure to denigration and social ostracism of varying degrees. The educational level of the adults tends to be quite limited. In the homes, there is likely to be a nearly complete absence of books, relatively few toys, and, in many instances, nothing except a few normal home-objects which may be adapted as playthings. In addition—particularly but not exclusively where relatively new in-migrants are concerned—there is a great deal of horizontal mobility. The result is a pattern of life that exposes a child to a minimum of direct contacts with the central channels of our culture. The conditions of social inequality, the absence of an accessible opportunity structure, and the frequent non-availability of successful adult male models create an atmosphere that is just not facilitating to individual development. Moreover, the everyday problems of living, particularly those of economic insecurity and a multiplicity of children, leave minimum time for the adults who may be present to assist the child in exploring the world, to reward him for successful completion of tasks, or to help him in the development of a differentiated self-concept. Even in homes which are not broken, the practical manifestations of economic marginality result in the father sometimes holding two jobs and having little time for interaction with the child. We have found in various studies that children from these circumstances have relatively few shared or planned family activities, again resulting in a narrowing of experience.

The implications of these environmental conditions for the development of the child can be appreciated in terms of Hunt's (1961) discussion of Piaget's developmental theories. He points out that, according to Piaget, ". . . the rate of development is in substantial part, but certainly not wholly, a function of environmental circumstances. Change in circumstances is required to force the accommodative modifications of schemata that constitute development. Thus, the greater the variety of situations to which the child must accommodate his behavioral structures, the more differentiated and mobile they become. Thus, the more new things a child has seen and the more he has heard, the more things he is interested in seeing and hearing. Moreover, the more variation in reality with which he has coped, the greater is his capacity for coping" (pp. 258–259). In essence, it is this richness and variety which a compensatory enrichment program must provide.

Previously, I have said that emphasis on the importance of variety in the environment implies the detrimental effects of lack of variety (Deutsch, 1963). I then postulated that a child from any circumstance who has been deprived of a substantial portion of the variety of stimuli to which he is maturationally capable of responding is likely to be deficient in the equipment required for school learning. This does not necessarily imply restriction in the quantity of stimulation; rather, it refers to a restriction in variety—that is, restriction to only a segment of the spectrum of stimulation potentially available. In addition to such restriction in variety, from the description of the slum environment, it might be postulated that the segments made available to children from that background tend to have poorer and less systematic ordering of stimulation sequences, thereby being less useful to the growth and activation of cognitive potential.

The most promising agency for providing environmental compensations is the school. It is through this institution, which reaches every child, that the requisite stimulation for facilitating learning, psychological maturation, and acculturation can be most efficiently organized and programmed. Yet it is now estimated that up to 60 per cent of lower class children are retarded two years or more in reading, by the time they leave the elementary school.

Before we place the entire responsibility on the school, however, an important fact must be noted. The overwhelming finding of studies on the relationship between social class and learning, school performance, and the like is that children from backgrounds of social marginality enter the first grade already behind their middle-class counterparts in a number of skills highly related to scholastic achievement. They are simply less prepared to meet the demands of the school and the classroom situation. Conversely, though, the school has failed to prepare to meet their needs. The failure of the educational institution to overcome the children's environmentally determined handicaps too often results in early failure, increasing alienation, and an increasingly greater gap between the lower class and middle-class youngsters as they progress through school. In other words, intellectual and achievement differences between lower class and middle-class children are smallest at the first grade level, and tend to increase through the elementary school years. It is here where the interaction between school and early environment, instead of having a facilitating influence, has a negative effect. While the school does not contribute to the initial problem (except through its effects on the previous generation), neither does it contribute to the overcoming of the initial handicaps.

CONTINUITY OF HOME AND SCHOOL EXPERIENCE

It would seem quite reasonable, in the light of this discussion and its supporting evidence, to better prepare the child to meet the school's demands before he enters the first grade, and before there has been an accumulation of failure experiences and maladaptive behavior. It would also seem eminently reasonable that the school should accept this responsibility. At the same time, it does not seem reasonable that an institution which so far has generally failed to meet its responsibility to this group should simply be given a mandate, without the incorporation of new and appropriate knowledge and techniques. Here is where the knowledge from the behavioral sciences can be put to its most effective use.

For example, all peoples have difficulties in spanning cultural discontinuities, and the entrance of the child into school for the first time places him in an environment which, in many respects, is discontinuous with his home. This discontinuity is minimal for the middle-class child, who is likely to have had the importance of school imprinted in his consciousness from the earliest possible age. For him, therefore, the school is very central and is continuous with the totality of his life experiences. As a result there are few incongruities between his school experiences and any others he is likely to have had, and there are intrinsic motivating and molding properties in the school situation to which he has been highly sensitized. Further, there is more likely to be contiguity in the school-faculty orientation with his home-family orientation. Failure can be interpreted to him in appropriate and familiar terms, and methods of coping with it can be incorporated, increasing the motivation or offering the necessary rewards, goals, or punishments to effect the desired change in performance.

For the lower class child there is not the same contiguity or continuity. He does not have the same coping mechanisms for internalizing success or psychologically surviving failure in the formal learning setting. If the lower class child starts to fail, he does not have the same kinds of operationally significant and functionally relevant support from his family or community—or from the school. Further, because of the differences in preparation, he is more likely to experience failure.

In this context, let us consider White's concept of competence motivation as a primary drive. The middle-class child comes to school prepared, for the most part, to meet the demands made on him. The expectations of his teachers are that he will succeed. As he confronts material that is congruent with his underlying skills, he is able to succeed; and thus he achieves the feeling of efficacy which White (1959) points out is so necessary to the "effectance motivation" which promotes continuing positive interaction with the environment. The lower class child, on the other hand, experiences the middle-class-oriented school as discontinuous with his home environment, and further, comes to it unprepared in the basic skills on which the curriculum is founded. The school becomes a place which makes puzzling demands, and where failure is frequent and feelings of competence are subsequently not generated. Motivation decreases, and the school loses its effectiveness.

INTERVENTION ENVIRONMENT

It is in the transitional years from the pre-school period through the elementary school years that the child is first subject to the influence and the requirements of the broader culture. It is then that two environments are always present for him: the home environment and the school environment. But it is also in these transitional (and especially in the pretransitional) years that the young organism is most malleable. Thus, that is the point at which efforts might best be initiated to provide a third—an intervention—environment to aid in the reconciliation of the first two. Such reconciliation is required because, especially for the child from a disadvantaged background, there are wide discrepancies between the home and school milieus. In the intervention environment, preventive and remedial measures can be applied to eliminate or overcome the negative effects of the discontinuities.

The importance of early intervention is underlined in the summary by Fowler (1962) of findings on cognitive learning in infancy and early childhood. He points out that seemingly minimal cognitive stimulation in the pre-school years, when organized appropriately to the capabilities of the child, can be highly effective in accelerating the development of intellectual functions.

Critical and optimal time periods for many aspects of development and learning in both humans and animals have long been studied. These concepts are always related to stimulation or interaction between the organism and the environment, and thus represent an important additional dimension when we discuss influences on development and behavior. Apparently, it is not sufficient merely to provide particular stimulation for the growing individual; it must be supplied at a special time, or within particular time limits, if it is to have the most desired effect. Thus, a program intended to compensate for environmental deprivation would be most effective if supplied at a particular stage in the life of the child.

Scott's (1962) summary of the relevant research information on critical stages in development indicates that the period of greatest plasticity is during the time of initial socialization. Since the bulk of the literature in this area is on animals, generalizations must be carefully confined. But seemingly, as one ascends the phylogenetic scale, there are greater ranges of time during which the organism has high levels of plasticity and receptivity. There is an insufficient body of data to hypothesize a most critical period for learning in the human child, and there are probably different critical or optimal periods for different functions. However, at about three or four years of age there is a period which would roughly coincide with the early part of what Piaget calls the "preoperational stage." It is then that the child is going through the later stages of early socialization; that he is required to focus his attention and monitor auditory and visual stimuli, and that he learns through language to handle simple symbolic representations. It is at this three- to four-year-old level that organized and systematic stimulation, through a structured and articulated learning program, might most successfully prepare the child for the more formal and demanding structure of the school. It is here, at this early age, that we can postulate that compensation for prior deprivation can most meaningfully be introduced. And, most important, there is considerably less that has to be compensated for at this age than exists when, as a far more complex and at least somewhat less plastic organism, the child gets to the first grade.

This position and its implications for specially organized early stimulation of the child find support in an article by

Bruner (1961) on cognitive consequences of sensory deprivation. He says: "Not only does early deprivation rob the
organism of the opportunity of constructing models of the
environment, it also prevents the development of efficient
strategies for evaluating information—for digging out what
leads to what and with what likelihood. Robbed of development in this sphere, it becomes the more difficult to utilize
probable rather than certain cues, the former requiring a more
efficient strategy than the latter." Bruner goes on to a discussion of non-specific transfer of training in which, I think, he
provides the most incontrovertible foundation for a structured,
systematic pre-school enrichment and retraining program
which would compensate, or attempt to compensate, for the deficiencies in the slum environment. His discussion is not of
slums or compensation, but in his pointing up the importance
of the "normally rich" environment, the serious cognitive consequences of the deprived environment are thrown into relief.
Bruner says, ". . . non-specific or generic transfer involves the
learning of general rules and strategies for coping with highly
common features of the environment." After pointing out that
Piaget ". . . remarks upon the fact that cognitive growth consists of learning how to handle the great informational transformations like reversibility, class identity, and the like" and
that Piaget speaks of these as "strategies for dealing with or,
better for creating usable information," Bruner proposes:
". . . that exposure to normally rich environments makes the
development of such strategies possible by providing intervening opportunity for strategic trial and error."

What Bruner talks about under "trial and error" requires a
certain level of motivation and exploratory efforts. I have previously discussed the possible role of early failure experiences
in influencing the motivational and goal orientations, and the
self-expectancies, of the lower class child. When the lower
class child gets into first grade, too frequently his cognitive,
sensory, and language skills are insufficiently developed to

cope with what for him are the complex and confusing stimuli offered by the school. It is the interaction of these motivational and maturational dynamics that makes it extremely important for society, through institutions such as the school, to offer the lower class child an organized and reasonably orderly program of stimulation, at as early an age as possible, to compensate for possible cognitive deficit.

EARLY ENRICHMENT PROGRAMS

The focus has been on deficit because of the general hypothesis that the experiential deprivations associated with poverty are disintegrative and subtractive from normative growth expectancies. The extent of academic failure and reading retardation associated with lower class status—and especially with minority group membership within the lower class—makes it imperative that we study the operational relationship between social conditions and these deficits, and the subsequent failure of the school to reverse the tendency toward cumulative retardation in the primary grades.

Our work has been directed particularly toward delineating the effects of conditions of life on cognitive structures. For an understanding of these relationships and the scientific development of enrichment programs, we have emphasized the role of specific social attributes and experiences in the development of language and verbal behavior, of concept formation and organization, of visual and auditory discrimination, of general environmental orientation, and of self-concepts and motivation; and of all of this to school performance. It is the areas mentioned which apparently are essential to the acquisition of scholastic skills, and around which a basic curriculum for early childhood should be developed. Pragmatically, this must be a program which successfully teaches disadvantaged children.

Examination of the literature yields no explanation or justification for any child with an intact brain, and who is not severely disturbed, not to learn all the basic scholastic skills. The failure of such children to learn is the failure of the schools to develop curricula consistent with the environmental experiences of the children and their subsequent initial abilities and disabilities.

As has been emphasized previously in this paper, a compensatory program for children, starting at three or four years of age, might provide the maximum opportunity for prevention of future disabilities and for remediation of current skill deficiencies. In addition, such a program might serve to minimize the effect of the discontinuity between the home and school environments, thereby enhancing the child's functional adjustment to school requirements.

For an early enrichment program, one model available is that developed by Maria Montessori (1870–1952) in the slums of Italy. Though her theoretical system (1959) need not be critically evaluated here, there is much in her technology that could productively be re-examined and incorporated in compensatory programs. Basically, this includes the organization of perceptual stimuli in the classroom, so that singular properties become more observable, one at a time, without the distraction of competing, overly complex elements. For example, materials used to convey and illustrate the concept of size and size differential are all the same color and shape. This maximizes the attentional properties of size, and minimizes competing elements. Use of such materials should make it possible for size discriminations to be learned more easily. This method is, of course, carried over to many fields, and the availability of such stimuli under the Montessori system gives the child an opportunity to select materials consistent with his own developmental capabilities. This makes possible success experience, positive reinforcement, and subsequent enhancement of involvement and motivation. The attention to the minutiae of learning, and the systematic exposure to new learning elements based on prior experience, could allow for the development of individualized learning profiles. This would be particularly appropriate for a compensatory program, where there is a great deal of variation in individual needs.

There is, however, a major variable which is apparently inadequately handled by this method, and that is language.

LANGUAGE DIFFICULTIES

Language can be thought of as a crucial ingredient in concept formation, problem-solving, and in the relating to and interpretation of the environment. Current data tend to indicate that class differences in perceptual abilities and general environmental orientation decrease with chronological age, while language differences tend to increase.

In a social-class-related language analysis, Basil Bernstein (1960), an English sociologist, has pointed out that the lower class tends to use informal language and mainly to convey concrete needs and immediate consequences, while the middle-class usage tends to be more formal and to emphasize the relating of concepts. This difference between these two milieus, then, might explain the finding in some of our recent research that the middle-class fifth grade child has an advantage over the lower class fifth grader in tasks where precise and somewhat abstract language is required for solution. Further, Bernstein's reasoning would again emphasize the communication gap which can exist between the middle-class teacher and the lower class child.

One can postulate that the absence of well-structured routine and activity in the home is reflected in the difficulty that the lower class child has in structuring language. The implication of this for curriculum in the kindergarten and nursery school would be that these children should be offered a great deal of verbalized routine and regulation, so that positive expectations can be built up in the child and then met. It can also be postulated that differences in verbal usage are directly attributable to the level of interaction of the child with the adult and, at this age to a lesser extent, with peers.

In observations of lower class homes, it appears that speech sequences seem to be temporally very limited and poorly structured syntactically. It is thus not surprising to find that a major focus of deficit in the children's language development is syntactical organization and subject continuity. But in analysis of expressive and receptive language data on samples of middle- and lower class children at the first and fifth grade levels, there are indications that the lower class child has more expressive language ability than is generally recognized or than emerges in the classroom. The main differences between the social classes seem to lie in the level of syntactical organization. If, as is indicated in this research, with proper stimulation a surprisingly high level of expressive language functioning is available to the same children who show syntactical deficits, then we might conclude that the language variables we are dealing with here are by-products of social experience rather than indices of basic ability or intellectual level. This again suggests a vital area to be included in any pre-school enrichment program: training in the use of word sequences to relate and unify cognitions.

A language training program would require the creation of a rich, individualized language environment, where words are repeatedly placed in a meaningful context, and where the child is allowed multiple opportunities for expressive language demonstrations as well as for receiving language stimuli under optimal conditions and being encouraged to make appropriate responses. More specifically, stress could be placed on the following areas orienting feedback, so that if the child says "give me the——" or "where is——," the teacher consciously instructs him in a complete sentence as to direction, location, placement, context, etc.: the systematic attempt to increase vocabulary; allowing the child to sort symbols, pictures, and artifacts with letters and words; verbal labelling practice; relating objects and experiences verbally, for example, constructing stories using specified objects and events; every child completing differently incomplete stories suggested by the teacher; reinforcing and encouraging the simultaneous articulation of motor behavior. Through the verbal area it is also possible to train memory, to some extent to train auditory discrimination, and to improve environmental orientation. However, it is not the purpose of this paper to go into a detailed description of potential enrichment procedures.

Working out compensatory programs is based on the assumption that retardation in achievement results from the interaction of inadequately prepared children with inadequate schools and insufficient curricula. This in turn is based on the contention that this large proportion of children is not failing because of inferior innate resources. Also implied is the assumption that one does not sit by and wait for children to "unfold," either on the intellectual or behavioral levels. Rather, it is asserted that growth requires guidance of stimulation, and that this is particularly valid with regard to the child who does not receive the functional prerequisites for school learning in the home. Hunt (1961) points out that ". . . the counsel from experts on child-rearing during the third and much of the fourth decades of the twentieth century to let children be while they grow and to avoid excessive stimulation was highly unfortunate." This is particularly true with regard to lower class children. We have found that, controlling for socioeconomic status, children with some pre-school experience have significantly higher intelligence test scores at the fifth grade than do children with no pre-school experience (Deutsch and Brown, 1964).

CONTINUITY OF PRE-SCHOOL AND SCHOOL PROGRAMS

But it is not necessary to consider special education programs only on the pre-school level, even though that is what has been emphasized here. Rather, to assure stability of progress, it would be desirable to continue special programs for several more years. The construction of a pre-school program does not absolve a community or a school system from the responsibility to construct an effective strategy for teaching the marginal youngster from kindergarten on. In fact, if there is to be a reversal of some of the sequelae associated with poverty discussed in this paper, programs must have continuity, at least through the period of the establishment of the basic scholastic learning skills. This means that it is necessary for the community to support kindergartens with reasonable enrollments and adequate equipment, as well as specialized training of staff. As far as the primary grades are concerned, the continuation of special programming through establishment of basic skills would involve probably the time through the third grade year. This level is used, because there is empirical reason to believe that levels of achievement for different social classes start their greatest divergence here. This is probably so because here the work begins to become less concrete and more abstract, more dependent on language symbolization, and, probably most important, more related to good reading skills. For these reasons, it would seem that the child from the pre-school and enriched kindergarten classes might best remain in a special ungraded sequence through the third grade level, a period in which he could be saturated with basic skill training, and not be allowed to move on until he has attained basic competence in the skills required by the higher grades. Such an ungraded school would also be of considerable interest theoretically, inasmuch as the child would be in its program through the preoperational stage delineated by Piaget. This should make it possible to devise a systematic curriculum that is consistent with the actual developmental levels of the child during the early childhood period.

Fowler (1962) points out that—

Few systematic methods have been devised for educating young children, especially in complicated subject matter.

We have in mind methods for simplifying and organizing the presentation of cognitive stimuli. Equally important, methods must be sufficiently flexible and play-oriented to be adaptable to the primary learning levels and personality organization characteristic of the infant and young child.

The advantages of utilizing the now relatively untapped "pre-school" years for cognitive education are, of course, manifest. Most obvious, is the availability of more years of childhood to absorb the increasingly complex technology of modern society, a technology already requiring many of the more productive years of development to acquire. A second is the less evident but more crucial possibility that conceptual learning sets, habit patterns, and interest areas, may well be more favorably established at early than at later stages of the developmental cycle.

SUMMARY

There are those people who seem to fear the word "cognitive," sometimes correctly, because they are reacting to the overstringent mechanical models of the past. These models are not what is meant. The potentiation of human resources through the stimulation of cognitive growth could represent a primary therapeutic method for developing positive self-attitudes and a meaningful self-realization. For the lower-class child especially, I would postulate that time is extremely valuable if the deficits are not to be cumulative and to permeate the entire functioning of the child.

The overgeneralized influence on some sections of early childhood education of the emphasis in the child guidance movement upon protecting the child from stress, creating a supportive environment, and resolving emotional conflicts has done more to misdirect and retard the fields of child care, guidance, and development than any other single influence. The effect has especially operated to make these fields ineffective in responding to the problems of integrating and educating the non-white urban child. These orientations have conceived of the child as being always on the verge of some disease process, and have assigned to themselves the role of protecting the child in the same manner that a zoo-keeper arranges for the survival of his charges. Too frequently a philosophy of protectiveness that asks only about possible dangers has prevailed over any question of potential stimulation of development. The attitude that perhaps helped to create this policy of protectionism can also be seen in the suburban "momism" that so many sociologists and psychoanalysts have commented on. The child is a far healthier and stronger little organism, with more intrinsic motivation for variegated experience and learning, than the overprotectionists have traditionally given him credit for.

As Fowler (1962) states further—

In harking constantly to the dangers of premature cognitive training, the image of the "happy", socially adjusted child has tended to expunge the image of the thoughtful and intellectually educated child. Inevitably, in this atmosphere, research (and education) in cognition has lagged badly, especially since the 1930s, not only for the early years of childhood but for all ages.

And as Hunt (1961) says: "The problem for the management of child development is to find out how to govern the encounters that children have with their environments to foster both an optimally rapid rate of intellectual development and a satisfying life."

A curriculum as discussed here should serve both for the primary prevention of the social deviancies associated with deprivation and for the stimulation of healthy growth and utilization of individual resources. This orientation would represent one effective method of offering opportunities to all peoples to overcome and break the chains of social and historical limitations that have been externally imposed on them. This of course has immediate significance to the current critical questions in both race relations and education in America.

BIBLIOGRAPHY

BERNSTEIN, BASIL, "Language and Social Class," *British Journal of Sociology,* 11:271–276, 1960.

BRUNER, J. S., "The Cognitive Consequences of Early Sensory Deprivation." In P. Solomon (ed.), *Sensory Deprivation.* Cambridge: Harvard University Press, 1961, pp. 195–207.

DEUTSCH, M., "Minority Group and Class Status as Related to Social and Personality Factors in Scholastic Achievement," *Society for Applied Anthropology Monograph* No. 2, 1960.

——— "The Disadvantaged Child and the Learning Process." In A. H. Passow (ed.), *Education in Depressed Areas.* New York: Columbia University, Teachers College Bureau of Publications, 1963, pp. 163–179.

DEUTSCH, M. and B. BROWN, "Social Influences in Negro-White Intelligence Differences," *Journal of Social Issues,* 24–35, April 1964.

FOWLER, W., "Cognitive Learning in Infancy and Early Childhood," *Psychological Bulletin,* 59:116–152, 1962.

HARRINGTON, M., *The Other America.* New York: Macmillan, 1962.

HUNT, J. McV., *Intelligence and Experience.* New York: Ronald, 1961.

MONTESSORI, MARIA, *Education for a New World.* Wheaton, Illinois: Theosophical Press, 1959.

SCOTT, J. P., "Critical Periods in Behavioral Development," *Science,* 138:949–955, 1962.

WHITE, R. W., "Motivation Reconsidered: The Concept of Competence," *Psychological Review,* 66:297–333, 1959.

5. A Pre-School Enrichment Program for Disadvantaged Children

Shirley Feldmann[1]

A program for the prevention of academic failure of children from disadvantaged urban areas has been undertaken by the Institute for Developmental Studies, under the direction of Dr. Martin Deutsch. The Institute is a research unit of the Department of Psychiatry of New York Medical College. Previous studies at the Institute investigating the cognitive, perceptual, and language skills of school-age children from disadvantaged areas indicated that the skill deficiencies which were found in such children might be reversible if enrichment programs could be offered at a pre-school level. It was argued that raising the skill levels of such children as well as helping them to learn how to learn might enable them to cope more easily with the curriculum offered them in early school years. Thus the progressing academic failure so often seen in such children might well be prevented.

Accordingly, in co-operation with the Board of Education and the Department of Welfare of New York City, a three-year demonstration and research nursery program for four-year-old children, sponsored by the Ford Foundation was

[1] Shirley Feldmann is now on the faculty of the City College of New York. This article originally appeared in *The New Era,* 45:3, 1964. The research presented was supported through the Ford Foundation and conducted at the Institute for Developmental Studies, Department of Psychiatry, New York Medical College.

initiated in 1962. This article is a brief report of its first year in operation.

The program was designed to explore the value of an enriched nursery program stressing particular areas of intellectual functioning as well as the school orientation and motivations necessary for adequate learning in the early elementary grades. There were two aspects of the program: (1) development and evaluation of the enriched curriculum; (2) evaluation of the effectiveness of that curriculum on later school achievement.

ENRICHED NURSERY CURRICULUM

The foundation for the enriched nursery program was the basic nursery curriculum supported by most early childhood specialists. The most salient feature of the new program was increased training for teachers and more participation for parents, in order to make both aware of the individual child's needs and deficiencies. Development of a positive self-image for the child was deemed crucial in orienting him toward learning. Thus, considerable time and effort was expended in enlisting teachers and parents to help bridge the home-school gap in establishing a good learning climate at school.

A second feature of the enriched nursery curriculum was its stress on language, concept formation, and perceptual discrimination. Those skills, considered basic for school learning, were often found to be deficient in the disadvantaged child, so they were given additional weight in the new program.

Both features of the program were reflected in the modifications and innovations made in the enriched curriculum during its first year, as described below.

In organizing the new program, the structural aspects of the curriculum, that is, the room arrangements and routines, were clearly specified for the child. An attempt was made to build concepts of order and space for him. It was also hoped that a simplified environment might help the child to focus attention on the curriculum itself rather than to have him distracted by irrelevant stimuli in the room.

Therefore, a simplified room environment was created through use of uncluttered equipment and furniture which was arranged in an orderly way in the room. Colors used for the equipment were also unified; for example, all the reds in the room were about the same shade of color. Further, each piece of equipment had a designated place which was clearly marked and made known to the children, so that they could replace any of it with ease.

It should be stressed that pressures were not exerted on any child to keep an orderly room. Rather, the thinking was that daily contact with an uncluttered environment might help him to learn about organization in time and space; tidiness was considered only a secondary benefit of this learning.

Similarly, because concepts of routine and order were poorly developed in the children, classroom routines were introduced slowly and explicitly through repeated motor demonstrations. Only after they were fully understood were verbal directions given alone. The child's concrete experience with routines were expected to make him aware of existing patterns of social action and to give him a sense of sequence and organization of activities. As routines were understood and became manageable for him, variations were introduced to build concepts of flexibility.

Another important learning was expected from the structural simplicity of the classroom. Skill in dealing with routines and room arrangement combined with growing acquisition of skills in other areas (to be described below) were expected to give the child a feeling of competence and self-esteem in the learning situation. With continued motivation toward learning, it was hoped that the child would then focus more successfully on the cognitive and creative aspects of the curriculum.

The curriculum itself was modified to touch more directly on the known skill deficiencies of the children. Primary stress was put on language, concept, and perceptual development, with development of positive self-image underlying each of those areas.

Development of self-image was reinforced by use of Negro and white dolls and use of full-length mirrors in the doll corner. Pictures of children with varying skin colors were hung in the classroom, books about Negro children were read, and snapshots of the children themselves in their classrooms were used for language activities.

In the language area, labeling of people and objects was emphasized first. Every opportunity was utilized to call each child by name, and to encourage use of the teacher's name. Use of the generalized name "teacher," or of a child's nickname, was discouraged, for it was thought that learning to distinguish one teacher or child from another might reinforce recognition of people as individuals with specific identifying features.

Similarly, all equipment was referred to by name to help sharpen the child's awareness of the relations of words to things. In choosing equipment or an activity, each child was required to verbalize and label his choice instead of simply pointing to it.

Activities to increase size and range of vocabulary and to encourage use of expressive language were also used. Individual teacher-child contacts served as the basis for initial expressive language. Class experiences and stories soon encouraged group language experiences. Then, activities such as use of two telephones in the doll corner, group finger plays, or songs gave the children opportunities for more extensive expression.

Stories and experiences were used to develop concepts such as size, shape, and color. Recognition and expansion of these concepts were then carried over into other activities. Even the cookies served during snack time were chosen for their shapes and colors.

Books served to develop both language and concepts. They

were chosen to have uncluttered format and stories, as well as to deal with experiences relevant to the child's world. Stories initially helped to reinforce the child's fund of information and to entertain him; later they also served as sources of new information. Favorite stories were tape-recorded by the teachers so that a child might on his own initiative listen through earphones to a particular story and at the same time follow it by watching the book. An effort was made to use different people to record the tapes so that the children could have varied experience with voice inflections and dialects.

Perceptual discrimination experiences were provided through graded use of standard equipment. For example, the easiest of a graded series of puzzles, a three or four object puzzle with each object one puzzle piece, was first introduced. Matching of pieces was reinforced by tactile experiences and by the verbal explanations of the teacher. Harder puzzles were used as the children seemed ready to make more complex discriminations.

The equipment was often grouped by particular physical characteristics. For example, the blocks were arranged on low shelves according to size and shape relationships, necessitating that their use and return to the shelves be a discrimination task.

Use of other equipment often required discriminations of size, shape, color, or number. One activity stressed color. The children were asked to take all objects of a particular color from a box of small objects. Another game, a miniature postal box, required shape discrimination. Each different slot took only a particular shaped slab; the child therefore had immediate feedback about the perceptual correctness of his choice.

Some discriminations were based on more complex understanding of concepts. In the doll corner the play food, the dishes, the cleaning equipment, etc., were each grouped separately to emphasize their particular functions.

In addition to their recreational aspects, music and rhythmic activities were the chief avenues for development of auditory discrimination skills. Dramatization of rhythms, through walking or running, gave the simplest discriminations. The children also made varying motor responses to high or low tones played on the xylophone. Action songs with repeated sequences helped to reinforce listening skills. Much later, many of the children were able to recognize the proper number of drum beats for their names.

Other familiar aspects of the nursery program also provided new experiences. Songs were also used for language development. Songs were introduced that stressed children's names or labels for familiar objects. Repetition of songs reinforced both word pronunciation and correct use of language.

The program, described above, was put into operation about a year ago. Classrooms in public schools in disadvantaged areas were only slightly modified to be made usable for the program. Fifteen children, with a group teacher and an assistant teacher, met for a two-hour session four days a week for the school year.

TEACHER TRAINING AND PARENT PARTICIPATION

As stated earlier, the teachers were the central figures in the program. For this reason, their training and preparation was intensive both before and during the program. In their seminars the teachers learned of the theoretical and experimental aspects of the program, and then helped to prepare the curriculum. Evaluations of the curriculum, the record-keeping, and the ongoing classroom observations were continued at weekly seminars after the nursery classes had begun. The importance of these seminars was underlined by the fact that the children's week was shortened by one day to provide meeting time for the teachers.

Parent participation was also vital to the program. Contact with the parents was maintained from the time of the child's registration for the program. Home visits were made by the teacher to gather firsthand knowledge of the child so as to ease his adjustment to school. Efforts were made to acquaint the parents with the program through group meetings, individual conferences, and observations of their children in the classroom. Workshops were also conducted to discuss with parents specific ways in which they could supplement the school program—for example, through reading stories at home.

EVALUATION

An evaluation program has been undertaken to investigate the effectiveness of the enriched curriculum in improving later school achievement. Control groups of children, chosen to participate in the testing but not in the enriched program, will be followed along with the experimental groups. Experimental and control groups participating in the first year of the program have been tested before and after the enriched nursery experience, and they will be retested in successive school years. The same plan will be followed in the next two years of the project.

Since the program is so recently under way, no results of the testing are yet available. Despite the lack of statistical evidence, teachers have already seen evidence of signs in the children at the end of the first year's program. They observed that the children were using short descriptive sentences instead of their former one-word requests. Descriptions of home happenings and verbalization of needs were more often noted, too. The children were reported to be able to listen and respond to verbal directions, with greatly increased attention spans.

Perhaps most important, gains were seen in increase of interest and enthusiasm toward school-oriented activities by both children and their parents. The children seemed more eager to participate in school activities—for example, to look at books and to take part in group experiences. The parents seemed more aware of their roles at home to prepare their children for school and of the potential that school holds for their children. Although such gains might well be difficult to measure objectively, the staff of the enrichment program felt that they were positive signs of an orientation toward learning that could only result in increased school achievement.

6. An Academically Oriented Pre-School for Culturally Deprived Children

Carl Bereiter, Siegfried Engelman, Jean Osborn, and Philip A. Reidford[1]

The experimental pre-school represents radical departures both in methods and in goals from any existing pre-school programs for the culturally deprived of which we are aware. These departures are based on two premises which we can defend only very briefly here. One premise is that mere enrichment of experience is not sufficient to enable the culturally deprived child to overcome his backwardness in skills necessary for later academic success. Analysis of available data on the effects of enrichment, principally that of Lee on the effects of selective migration on Negro intelligence[2] and that of Kirk on the effects of early education of the mentally retarded,[3] indicates that the most that can be hoped for is an average gain of one year in mental age for each year of enriched educational

[1] The authors are members of the Institute for Research on Exceptional Children at the University of Illinois. The material in this article was originally presented as part of a symposium at the American Educational Research Association Convention in Chicago, February 12, 1965. The research reported herein was supported through the Cooperative Research Program of the Office of Education, United States Department of Health, Education, and Welfare.

[2] Lee, E. S., "Negro Intelligence and Selective Migration: A Philadelphia Test of the Klineberg Hypothesis," *American Sociological Review*, 16:227–233, 1951.

[3] Kirk, S. A., *Early Education of the Mentally Retarded*. Urbana: University of Illinois Press, 1958.

experience. From this it is a matter of simple arithmetic to show that a four-year-old child who is already a year retarded in the development of verbal intellectual abilities cannot be expected to overcome his deficit through a year or two of enriched experience. Indeed, he should never entirely overcome his deficit, even with continuing enrichment.

For this reason we were led to reject the approach of the typical nursery school, which appears to be based upon mimicry of those aspects of the culturally privileged home environment which are deemed significant for intellectual and personality growth. A more fruitful approach appeared to be that of selecting specific and significant educational objectives and teaching them in the most direct manner possible, as is done in the intermediate and secondary school grades.

The second premise has to do with the selection of those educational objectives. It is no news that the outstanding deficiencies of culturally deprived children are in the area of language. Language covers such an enormous territory, however, that setting up language development as an objective for pre-school education narrows the field hardly at all. The field can be narrowed considerably by separating out those aspects of language which mainly serve purposes of social communication from those aspects which are more directly involved in logical thinking. The former include lexical terms —nouns, verbs, and modifiers—and idiomatic expressions. The outstanding feature of the latter aspect of language is the manipulation of statement patterns according to grammatical and syntactical rules.

This is an artificial division, of course, but it has some value for curriculum planning. A great deal of effort can be and often is expended in building up the child's repertoire of idioms and concrete words and teaching him conventional usage patterns. All of this mainly serves to enable the child to get along better in the language environment. It is much like what a tourist gets out of studying a list of useful words and phrases in a foreign language. A child may be able to accumulate a great deal of learning of this kind and still be unable to reason verbally, to draw inferences from statements, and to generate the statements that are called for by questions. To do this requires a mastery of the formal aspects of language.

Our second premise was that training in the formal, structural aspects of language would have more value in the improvement of academic aptitude for culturally deprived children than would training directed toward "getting along" linguistically. From our earlier work in teaching concrete logical operations it became evident that culturally deprived children do not just think at an immature level: many of them do not think at all. That is, they do not show any of the mediating processes which we ordinarily identify with thinking. They can not hold onto questions while searching for an answer. They can not compare perceptions in any reliable fashion. They are oblivious of even the most extreme discrepancies between their actions and statements as they follow one another in a series. They do not just give bad explanations. They can not give explanations at all, nor do they seem to have any idea of what it is to explain an event. The question and answer process which is the core of orderly thinking is completely foreign to most of them.

The curriculum that we worked out, starting from the two premises discussed above, is an academically oriented one, using direct instruction that focuses upon the basic information processes that are necessary for thinking. Three content areas were chosen. One is basic language training and the other two are reading and arithmetic. The same information processes are involved in all three areas, but their application is different. These three areas were seen therefore, not as different "subjects" in the traditional sense, but as different areas of application in which a child must be proficient in order to succeed in the elementary school.

At the present time our work is largely developmental.

We have not yet run a controlled comparison of the effects of our program with the effects of other possible treatments. Rather, our present concerns include: (1) analysis of the formal characteristics of language, reading, and arithmetic that are relevant to young culturally deprived children, (2) translating these into instructional goals, (3) discovering feasible means of carrying on direct instruction with young culturally deprived children, (4) determining how much of what we would like to teach actually can be taught to children of this kind, and (5) assessing the rate of learning which can be achieved.

Our subjects are fifteen children selected in the following manner. Public school teachers in a low income, almost totally Negro district made visits to the homes of children in their classes. They were asked to note families in which there was a four-year-old child, in which the older sibling whom they had in class showed educational problems, and where the home environment struck them as particularly deprived. Of the families approached, all but one agreed to send their child. We rejected two children—a pair of identical twins who were almost completely non-verbal, unmanageable, and showed indications of severe brain injury. Thus, the fifteen children represent a fairly unbiased selection from the lower stratum of a culturally deprived ghetto.

The school runs for two hours a day, five days a week. The typical school day consists of three twenty-minute sessions, one each devoted to language, arithmetic, and reading instruction. These periods are separated by one half-hour period for refreshments and singing and a shorter period of relatively unstructured play activity. For the instructional sessions the children work in groups of four or five. Each subject has its own teacher, who works with each of three groups of children in turn, as in a high school. Groups are constituted on the basis of over-all rate of progress, with children being frequently shifted from one group to another as their relative achievement level shifts. Two children whose learning rate is far below that of the others compose a fourth group which receives training in all three subjects from a single teacher. This arrangement is required by scheduling problems, however, and is not a matter of preference. In a larger school with more teachers it would be possible to accommodate even such retarded children in the regular program.

The school as a whole is run in a highly task-oriented, nononsense manner. Full participation of all children in the learning tasks is treated as a requirement to which the children must conform (much like the hand-washing requirement in a conventional nursery school) rather than as a developmental goal toward which the children are allowed to progress at their own rate. Emphasis is placed upon effort, attention, and mastery, but not upon competition, as is so damagingly done in many of our more achievement-oriented elementary schools. It may be mentioned in passing that the morale and self-confidence of the children appears to be very high and that there are relatively few signs of psychological stress.

We will discuss in detail the three separate instructional programs and the achievements of the children in them after three months of work. Here, by way of a more general indication of effectiveness of the program, we may consider changes in scores on three subtests of the Illinois Test of Psycholinguistic Abilities (ITPA). The auditory-vocal automatic and the auditory-vocal association subtests were administered to the children several days before the school began. The auditory-vocal automatic is essentially a test of ability to use grammatical inflections for the formation of plurals, comparatives, and tenses. It is a test on which culturally deprived children have been found to be especially subnormal. The auditory-vocal association subtest consists of simple verbal analogies and has been found to be highly correlated with Stanford-Binet scores. At the time of first testing the children had a median chronological age of 4-3. They were as a whole over a year retarded on both subtests. Not one child, in fact, was performing up to his age level on either subtest.

Approximately three weeks after the beginning of the school the full ITPA was administered. On the two subtests that had been given previously, median scores went up nine and ten months. (Medians are used throughout, because the existence of some scores that were below norms for the subtests made calculation of means impossible.)

Three months after the beginning of school selected subtests of the ITPA were again administered. Gains of thirteen months over pretest scores were obtained on both subtests, with gains of four and three months respectively over those obtained on the first retest. Retesting was also done at this time on another subtest: vocal encoding. This is a relatively unstructured test. Subjects are presented various objects and told to "tell me all about it." Scores are based on the number of different appropriate things that the subject says. This subtest was of interest as a check on the possibility that direct training in language patterns might have little or no transfer value to language usage in unstructured situations. The results showed, however, that performance of this freer, more "creative" type improved more markedly than any other—a median gain of fifteen months, bringing the group as a whole up near normal on this scale. Since this test gets fairly directly at the social uses of language, it would appear, paradoxically enough, that the best way to teach young culturally deprived children to verbalize more freely and expressively (which is the major concern of many pre-school programs for the culturally deprived) is to ignore the matter and concentrate on more fundamental language processes.

In terms of the traditional achievement quotients, these children gained approximately 20 points in three months in three highly significant language areas. On two of them they are now close to normal. We do not, however, regard these results as the most important indications of the effectiveness of the program. The more specific achievements in language, reading, and arithmetic, to be reported in the following sections, indicate more directly what it is that these children have been able to accomplish. Judged by absolute standards, it will be found that most of these children are still a long way from mastery of language, reading, and arithmetic. On the other hand, their progress in three months' time seems to compare rather favorably with that of culturally deprived children in the first grade, and these children are two years younger. In this sense the children are academically precocious, and in their general attitude and approach to learning this is how they act. There is every indication that the children will be able to maintain their present rate of academic progress. How much of this will be reflected in more global measure of intellectual ability remains to be seen, but it is more or less beside the point. Our strategy, as indicated earlier, is not to try to do everything in an attempt to increase intellectual abilities across the board, but to concentrate our efforts on what seems most significant for academic success.

STRUCTURAL LANGUAGE TRAINING

Almost every experimental pre-school program for culturally deprived children that we know of makes some serious effort, however informal, to improve children's language abilities. Though methods vary from program to program, there is an order of emphasis on different aspects of language behavior which appears to be almost universally accepted. Primary emphasis is given to encouraging the children to make fuller use of whatever language skills they possess—to merely getting the children to talk, in some fashion or other. Then, in descending order of emphasis, attention is given to vocabulary building, improving pronunciation, and finally to improving grammatical structure. The last two are often given no methodical attention at all, but are expected to emerge as natural consequences of progress in the first two.

We established a program which essentially reverses the usual order of emphasis. The program's major concern is the acquisition of grammatical statement patterns and a grasp of the logical organization of these patterns. Precise pronunciation is seen as a critical requirement for mastery of grammatical structure, for even in our relatively uninflected language a good deal of grammatical structure is mediated by little affixes, variations, and particles which cannot be differentiated by the blurred pronunciation typical of culturally deprived children. The child who says "Ih bwah" for "This is a block" is in a poor position to understand, much less communicate, such contrasting statements as "This is not a block," "These are blocks," and "These are not blocks." For this reason, and not because we were interested in niceties of diction, we have given a great deal of emphasis to perfecting pronunciation.

As for vocabulary development, we have allowed much of it to occur as an incidental outcome of work on grammatical structure. Where direct teaching of concepts has been done, it has been concerned with concepts chosen because of their value in organizing experience and in making logical distinctions—for instance, inclusive class concepts such as *people, food,* and *vehicles.*

Perhaps our most radical departure from tradition has been our treatment of the child's already established language patterns. It seems to have been taken for granted by other educators that one must begin by encouraging the child to make the fullest possible use of the language he already possesses before one may set about improving it. Our estimation of the language of culturally deprived children agrees, however, with that of Bernstein, who maintains that this language is not merely an underdeveloped version of standard English, but is a basically non-logical mode of expressive behavior

which lacks the formal properties necessary for the organization of thought.[4] From this point of view, the goal of language
training for the culturally deprived could be seen as not that
of improving the child's language but rather that of teaching
him a different language which would hopefully replace the
first one, at least in school settings. The two languages share
lexical elements and these we made use of, but apart from this
we proceeded much as if the children had no language at all.
This led us naturally to adopt many of the techniques of
modern oral methods of foreign language teaching, which, as
Ausubel has pointed out, proceed upon the same assumption.[5] While we have not actively suppressed children's use of
their "native" language in ordinary social intercourse, neither
have we gone out of our way to encourage it. Rather, we have
strived to get the children to extend the language patterns they
were being deliberately taught into less structured social
situations.

INITIAL LANGUAGE ABILITY

The success of the language training program, at this early
date, at least, must be judged against the language abilities
which the children brought with them. These children exhibited the severe and general language impoverishment which
has been described by Deutsch and others.[6] This is borne out
by the pretest data, which showed them to be on the average
a year to a year-and-a-half retarded in language development.

When the children first arrived, they had, as expected, a

---

[4] Bernstein, Basil, "Language and Social Class," *British Journal of Sociology*, 11:271–276, 1960.

[5] Ausubel, D. P., "Adults versus Children in Second-Language Learning:
Psychological Considerations," University of Illinois, Bureau of Educational
Research, n.d. (Mimeograph.) Ausubel criticizes audiolingual methods for
this fact, but it should be recognized that this criticism applies to their use
with older students who have already mastered a first language which has
considerable transfer value to the second.

[6] Deutsch, M., "The Role of Social Class in Language Development and
Cognition," *American Journal of Orthopsychiatry*.

minute repertoire of labels to attach to the objects they used or saw every day. All buildings were called "houses," most people were called "you." Although Urbana is in the midst of a rural area, not one child could identify any farm animals. As obvious as their lack of vocabulary was their primitive notion of the structure of language. Their communications were by gesture (we later discovered that one boy could answer some questions by shaking his head, but that he did not realize that a positive shake of the head meant yes), by single words (Teacher: "What do you want?" Child: "Doll"), or a series of badly connected words or phrases. ("They mine." "Me got juice.")

The pronunciation of several of the children was so substandard that, when they did talk, the teachers had no notion of what they were saying. One of the brighter girls would ramble on and on, using a lot of poorly enunciated words and loosely connected phrases, but in an order that made little or no sense to any of the teachers or (as we learned later) to her mother.

Typical of their social non-use of language was the time it took to teach the children each others' names, and for them to learn to use these names in playing with each other.

Dramatic as these deficiencies are, they impressed us as much less significant than other, more subtle differences that appeared as we began trying to teach them. Although most of the children could follow simple directions like, "Give me the book," they could not give such directions themselves, not even repeat them. Without exaggerating, we may say that these four-year-olds could make no statements of any kind. They could not ask questions. Their ability to answer questions was hampered by the lack of such fundamental requirements as knowing enough to look at the book in order to answer the question, "Is the book on the table?"

TEACHING PROCEDURES

How can a four-year-old child be taught the logical structure of our language? The basic technique we have used is
similar to what foreign language teachers call "pattern drill."
The children learn basic statement patterns and how to answer
the fundamental questions about those patterns.

For example, in the teaching of "*big*" and "*little*," the following standard procedure was observed.

REPETITION OF THE VERBAL STATEMENT CONTAINING THE
CONCEPT
    Teacher: "This block is big."
    Child: "This block is big."

LOCATION OF CONCEPT
    Teacher: "Show me the block that is big."
              The child touches the big block.

VERBAL STATEMENT
    Teacher: "Tell me about the block."
    Child: "The block is big."

Rhetorical questions are used at every stage, "Is this the big
block?" These questions demonstrate the questions inferred in
every statement. Since the children did not have a storehouse
of statement and question patterns, in which, by varying the
subject and predicate to match the topic at hand, they could
communicate an observation or ask a question, much time was
spent learning such patterns.

After learning *big,* and in the same fashion, *little,* they
learned that these antonyms were comparatives, that if a big
block and a little block were drawn on the chalkboard, the
big block could become the little block if the little one was
erased and an even bigger block drawn next to the remaining
block.

Antonyms were also used to teach positive and negative statements and the deductions inherent in them. After each child learned the positive statement pattern, "This block is big," the question was asked, "Can you show me the block that is *not* big?" Not one of the children could make the deduction that something that is not big was little. So, again, the patterns were repeated: "This is the one that is not big." "Show me the one that is not big." "Tell me about this block." "This block is not big; it is little." This pattern was soon condensed to, "Show me the one that is *not* little."

Positive and negative statements had immediate application to the school discipline—Teacher: "Do we run down the hall?" Child: "No, we do not run down the hall. We walk down the hall." By substituting various subjects (balls, people, sticks, blocks, voices, dolls) and predicate pairs (fat-skinny, tall-short, long-short, loud-soft, fast-slow, heavy-light, soft-hard), the children were able, by varying the vocabulary, to apply these statement patterns to many situations.

In all of the work with statement patterns, special emphasis is given to achieving clear pronunciation of the particles which distinguish one statement from others that may involve the same lexical elements. If the child cannot clearly pronounce the words "is" and "in" in repeating, "The crayon is *in* the box," he will have difficulty grasping the difference between this statement and "The crayon is *on* the box" or "The crayon is not *in* the box." Many of the important logical distinctions in our language are conveyed by small words or particles which are easily slurred over: *and* versus *or, than* versus *and, big* versus *bigger, is* versus *isn't.*

The children were not able to pronounce, use, or understand the functions of prepositions and conjunctions in a sentence. Prepositions selected to be learned were *in, on, above, under, beside, between, in front of, in back of.* A child was instructed to sit on a table; if he didn't do this correctly, the teacher helped him and said, "You are sitting on the

table." The child and teacher repeated the statement. The
teacher repeated the statement. The teacher asked the child
"Where are you sitting?" The child would say, "On the table."
Teacher: "Now say the whole thing." Child: "I am sitting on
the table." Eventually, one child was able to give another child
the orders to sit under the table, stand beside the table, hold
a hand above the table, etc. In translating words into actions
the underlying logic of grammatical forms becomes apparent
to the child so long as the specified or implied operation is
physically possible. In correctly following an instruction to sit
under the table, the child demonstrates to himself the connection between word and action. The next and more difficult
step is to have the child describe the relationship between action and word. The teacher puts a pencil between a red block
and a green block; the child must describe the action. Tasks
of this type give children practice in manipulating the verbal
machinery necessary to transfer words into action, action into
words.

In teaching the conjunctions *and* and *or,* we placed objects
such as toy furniture on the table. The child was requested to
pick up a chair and a stove. He was asked to tell in sentence
form what he had: "I have a chair and a stove." The process
was repeated with *or.* Soon the students were giving each other
the orders, with the teacher requesting one child to give another an *and* order, then an *or* order. Children who had
difficulty differentiating between the two words were given the
instruction, "When you hear *and* it means you take two things;
when you hear *or* you must decide on one." (One boy, when
given an *and* instruction paused with his hand above the
objects and said aloud, *"And* means two, I got to pick up two
things," and proceeded to pick up two objects.)

The lessons on *and* and *or* extended to using sentences in
which the instruction was "Pick up a table and a chair and a
refrigerator," thus extending the number of things that could
be obtained by using more *ands.* Next, requests were given to

pick up all the white blocks and all the yellow blocks, introducing the notion of groups connected by *and*. All the above lessons were repeated with *or*. Then, *and* was taught as a conjunction connecting words that describe one object: "She has a red and white dress." "This cookie is big and round." Now the children are learning about the reversibility of the subjects around *and*. The teacher says, "I have a green block and a red block. Can you tell me another way I can say it? I have a red block and a green block. Is this saying the same thing?" This is a good example of a word pattern which has direct transfer to and from a mathematical concept that was being taught in the arithmetic class: $3 + 1 = 4$; $1 + 3 = 4$.

This kind of practice does relatively little in expanding concept formation when compared to enriched play situations, field trips, and extensive story-reading. What it does do is teach the children directly those elements of vocabulary which they would have difficulty learning from casual experience.

As we have said, straight vocabulary teaching is not a major goal in this program; when we do teach vocabulary, the words are not chosen so much for their social usefulness as for their value in making logical distinctions and in organizing experience. On this basis we decided to devote a good deal of attention to the teaching of colors and the more inclusive class names. In teaching color the classification rule, "If it looks the same, it is the same; if it's not the same, it's different," became most useful. We started with blocks and pieces of colored paper. If two red blocks were placed side by side they belonged to the same classification, red, and therefore had the same name. If two blocks, one red, and one green, were placed side by side, the statement, "If this one is red, this one is not red," could be made even if the child did not know the second color. This rule gave the children a means of discriminating and matching the properties of color in objects. Blocks, picture books, the children's own clothing, their toys, the juice they drank, the cars they rode to school in, were all used to teach color names.

In teaching categories of objects we used pictures in books, toys and furniture in the room, drawings on the chalkboard, and the children themselves. They learned a system for classifying objects, while simultaneously expanding their repertoire of concepts and vocabulary. When the children learned cow, horse, pig, sheep, rooster, and duck, they also learned that these were all farm animals, and that they were called farm animals because they lived on a farm. They learned that apples, bread, potatoes, and butter were food, and that what they ate was defined as food. Similarly they learned about the categories of people, furniture, clothes, toys, wild animals, birds, buildings, letters, and numbers, and the names of many members of these groups.

The gains in scores on ITPA subtests, reported in the introduction, provide one form of evidence of the effectiveness of the program. Of the three subtests cited, only the auditory-vocal automatic subtest can be construed as showing direct teaching effects, however. It tests mastery of grammatical inflections which, in English, are so few in number that it would be impossible to teach grammatical usage without "teaching for the test." The other two subtests may be taken to indicate generalization of language learning. The analogy form employed in the auditory-vocal association subtest was never employed in teaching, and the unstructured describing behavior called for in the vocal encoding subtest was quite foreign to our instructional procedures.

In the *Color Test* the children were required to name the colors of squares on the color chart. The teacher pointed to the squares in random order and the child was required to name the color. A plus indicates success on the first trial. Although none of the children knew even the basic colors when they started school, all but one showed fairly complete mastery of colors at the end of three months.

Items on the *Prepositions Test* required the child to accomplish two things in order to earn a plus—follow an instruction, and give a correct verbal description. Example: Teacher: "Put the scissors in front of the box." The child had to put the scissors in front of the box and then, in response to the question, "Tell me, where are the scissors?" the child had to make a complete statement equivalent to "The scissors are in front of the box." This kind of statement-making, which was beyond all the children at the outset, may be seen to have been quite thoroughly mastered.

The *Categories Test* required the child to give the proper category word when shown pictures of various objects within a given category. For example, in the category, *furniture,* the child was shown pictures of a table, a chair, a lamp, a bed, and a chest of drawers, and asked, "What is the word that we can use that means all of these things?" He was then asked, "What do we do with furniture?" To be given credit for a correct answer he had to know the category word and to be able to make a general statement about the category on the first trial.

The *Identity Statement* is a test of the child's ability to understand the structure as apart from the content of a sentence. The teacher drew identical figures, pointed to the first and then to the second as she said, "If this ⌔ is a blurp, is this ⌔ a blurp?" If the child said "Yes," it was assumed he understood the principle of labeling: if two things look the same, they have the same name. The next task involves two different figures, the question is the same, "If this ⌔ is a blurp, is this ⬭ a blurp?" Passing criterion: correct response on first trial.

For the *And Test,* the child was asked to pick up a green block and a red block, then asked, "What's another way of saying it?" If the child picked up both blocks and was able to restate the instruction to "pick up a red block and a green block" he passed both sections of the *And Test*.

For the *Or Test,* the child had to pick up one object when told to "Pick up a red block or a green block." If he could do this and restate the instruction to "pick up a red block or a green block" he passed the *Or Test*.

All children could handle the meanings of *and* and *or* adequately, though none of them could respond appropriately to *or* previous to instruction. Reversal or commutation of elements about *and* and *or* was not yet fully mastered, but work on it had only begun at the time of testing.

For the *Size Test* the child was shown two books and asked which one was bigger. To pass he had to point to the bigger one and say, "This is bigger than that one." The other two parts of the test were similar in form.

In the *Statements Test* the child was shown a picture with two squirrels, one in a tree and one on the ground. The teacher, pointing to the squirrel in the tree, asked "Where is this squirrel?" The correct response was, "The squirrel is in the tree." Next, the teacher pointed to the squirrel on the ground. "Is this squirrel in the tree?" The correct answer was "No, this squirrel is not in the tree." If the child said, "This squirrel is on the ground," he was asked to give the "not" answer. To pass, the child had to make two complete statements, but was allowed to rephrase incomplete statements into complete sentences.

What these results indicate is that all the children have begun to operate at the statement level, which is to say that they have begun to master those formal grammatical patterns which are lacking even in the speech of their parents. Although this kind of linguistic achievement is commonplace among culturally privileged four-year-olds, and therefore tends to be taken for granted when it is observed, we have found that this is the single most impressive achievement of these children in the eyes of experienced teachers of culturally deprived children—the fact that they speak in sentences. From our point of view, however, it is not the speaking in sentences itself which is important, but what speaking in sentences enables the children to do. It enables the children to "unpack" meaning from statements, to convey meanings which they otherwise could not, and to draw inferences which carry them beyond the immediately given facts.

TEACHING ARITHMETIC THROUGH LANGUAGE OPERATIONS

The new mathematics treats arithmetic as a system of statements and statement forms. In the present project, we have carried the "new math" orientation even further; we have endeavored to teach arithmetic as a *language*. This is not a completely arbitrary position. Mathematics is a system of language, and it shares four fundamental assumptions with statements in everyday language.

(1) The first is the assumption of classification and transition. If you can make identical statements about two things they are the same; they can be classified together. Also, if two things are the same as a third, they are the same as each other.

(2) The second major assumption is what might be called the reality assumption. The statement, "The coins are in the box," implies an operation. It implies that if, for instance, you assemble more than one coin and a box, you can create a model of the statement, "The coins are in the box." So it is with statements in arithmetic such as $3 + 2 = 5$. The statement implies that if you begin with three anythings and acquire two more anythings, you will have a sum of five anythings. The reality assumption is quite the same for both the statement that is capable of being true or false and the statement in arithmetic. *Neither specify a physical operation; both, however, imply one.*

(3) The third common assumption is that both arithmetic statements and everyday language statements imply questions

and answers. "The coins are in the box," implies such questions as "Where are the coins?" . . . "Are the coins in the box?" . . . "Are the coins under the box?" . . . and so forth. The arithmetic statement, $3 + 2 = 5$, implies analogous questions. "Three plus two equals how many?" . . . "Does three plus two equal five?" . . . and so forth. Note that these questions and answers derive from the statement and not from the individual components of the statement. A set of questions and answers derives even when the statement is reduced to a propositional function, such as "$A + B = C$" or "The glack is in the gleep." The statement has a meaning which *cannot* be reduced to the meaning of the constituent elements. The statement, therefore, is in this respect the basic unit of the language.

(4) The final shared assumption is that parts which compose a statement have a meaning. *Three* has a meaning in terms of counting. *In* has a meaning in terms of the position of objects.

What does all this mean? Simply that the extent to which arithmetic and everyday language share assumptions is the extent to which arithmetic is nothing more than a foreign language. *To this extent it can be taught as a foreign language.* However, the analogy between the two types of statements is not precise. Although arithmetic statements share every assumption that characterizes everyday language, they possess an additional assumption which is not shared by statements in everyday language. *Arithmetic statements such as $3 + 2 = f$ provide for their own completion.* If one understands how the system works, he can complete a statement without knowing the completed statement in advance. The statement implies that one can translate the statement into an operation and then *count* to discover the completed statement. Furthermore, any of the five elements in the statement can be eliminated and the completed statement can be discovered.

Because arithmetic statements provide for their own completion, arithmetic cannot be treated precisely as a foreign language. The extent to which the presentation should be different is the extent to which the content is different. In other words, arithmetic is primarily a language; however, many arithmetic statements possess a peculiar property.

Our presentation began with the individual concepts that make up a statement. The individual members were defined in terms of counting. The signs were defined in terms of the operations they imply. Thus, the symbol + is read as "plus" but is translated as the operation, "Get more." Similarly, the = sign tells you to *end up*. Next, after concepts we presented the fundamental statement forms of the arithmetic language. We began with the identity statement. The parallel in everyday language would be such a statement as "This is a stove." In a sense, it says no more than the word *stove,* and yet it is capable of generating a series of questions and answers that cannot derive from the word alone. So it is with arithmetic. After the dust has settled, the statement "A + 0 = A" says no more than "A," and yet it is capable of generating a series of questions and answers.

The identity statements were taught as a rote pattern. "One plus zero equals one, two plus zero equals two," and so forth. The purpose of presenting statements in the counting order was to establish the parallel between the identity statement and the familiar counting elements. We wanted the child to understand that since the identity statement held for every number in the familiar counting series, it should hold for any new numbers that are introduced.

After the identity relationship came the basic non-identity conclusion. These parallel the pattern in everyday language, "If it's not hot it must be ———." "If it's not the same it must be ———." The basic non-identity conclusion in arithmetic holds that a non-identity statement is not an identity statement. Or, stated operationally, "If 1 + 0 = 1, 1 + 1 can't equal 1. It equals 1 more than 1—2." The non-identity conclusion was again presented as a pattern, in an attempt to demonstrate that if the +1 conclusion holds for every number in the familiar series, it should hold for any new number introduced into the series.

In connection with these tasks, the basic substitution assumption of arithmetic was introduced as an operation. "If A = 2 it means that you can put a 2 wherever you have an A." The final language-type parallel that was taught was the reversible-element notion. Some elements in a compound statement can be reversed without affecting either the questions the statement generates or the answers to these questions. In arithmetic, this is the so-called commutative law: a + B = B + a. We presented the law as a language task. "What's another way of saying 2 + 0? 0 + 2."

All arithmetic problems were presented as "questions." An algebraic type symbol was introduced as the question asker: 3 + 2 = a. The children were taught to read the problem first, then translate it into a question, then answer the question. If the children did not know the answer to the question, they were taught how to "figure it out." This involves first understanding what question the problem is asking, then somehow translating the problem into a counting operation. We noted earlier that the open statement in arithmetic implies a physical operation but does not specify one. For several reasons, we choose a finger-counting operation as the "reality parallel" of the statement. "Start with 3" means to hold up three fingers on the left hand. "Get 2 more," meaning to hold up two fingers on the right hand. By counting the extended fingers, the child arrives at the answer, which hopefully is five. Since the total number of fingers is five, he can, according to substitution assumption, put a five in place of the *a*. Thus, 3 + 2 = 5.

A number of minor conventions had to be introduced to

make the system operational—for instance, the idea that the answer to the question, "How many?" is always the name of a single number, not a series of numbers. Also, since the basic questions were sometimes presented visually, the children had to know how to "read" the statement. Therefore, the symbols 0, 1, 2, 3, 4, 5, 6, 10, +, and = were introduced, together with several symbols for "how many."

The extent to which the language of arithmetic parallels the language of everyday usage is the extent to which the culturally deprived child should have difficulty with the type of arithmetic presentation we used. Obviously, a child who does not understand the statement, "It's not in the box if it's on top of the box," is going to be at a disadvantage when he tries to understand the statement, "1 + 1 can't equal 1, if 1 + 0 = 1." Similarly, he's going to have trouble understanding the relation between arithmetic questions and answers if he doesn't understand the relationship between questions and answers in everyday language.

Our children had a very slow start. Only two of them came to the school with any knowledge of counting. None could repeat a simple arithmetic statement, such as 2 + 3 = 5. None could read symbols. Only two or three knew that the answer to the question "How many?" is a single number. Only about a third of them knew the concepts *same* and *different*. None could reverse elements in a statement, 2 + 0 (which, by the way, is probably the most difficult task they have encountered in arithmetic).

Despite the initial deficit of our children, they are presently showing good progress.

The children were tested on three major areas of achievement—verbal tasks, visual tasks, and more difficult tasks—the solution of which involves the interplay of visual, motor, and vocal elements. Tasks were presented in roughly the order of difficulty.

TASK 1: Children were asked to count as far as they could, and they were encouraged to keep going if they stopped. All but one child counted to 10 without a mistake.

TASK 2: Children were asked, "What comes after one?" . . . "What comes after two?" . . . etc. Each incorrect response was corrected before the next question was presented. The slowest group did not perform as well as the other two, but the poorest performer missed only three, and nine children did perfectly.

TASK 3: Children were presented with a mathematical statement, such as $2 + 2 = 4$. They were then asked "Two plus how many equals four?" The children in the top two groups had no trouble with this task.

TASK 4: The identity series was presented in the counting order, "One plus zero equals ———, two plus zero equals ———." All but one child went through the entire 1–10 series without a mistake.

TASK 5: Identity statements were presented out of context. "Tell me, what would four plus zero equal? . . ." The children in the slowest group had more trouble with this item. This suggests that though they can produce the identity pattern, as in *Task 4,* the slowest children have not yet grasped it as a rule.

TASK 6: Plus-one problems were presented in the counting order. "One plus one equals ———, two plus one equals ———" and so on through "nine plus one equals ———." Highly variable success is shown on this task.

TASK 7: Plus-one statements were presented out of the context of the counting order. A child in both of the top two groups, as well as two children in the slowest group, had trouble with this task.

TASK 8: Children were presented with a statement such as "Eight plus two," then asked, "What's another way of saying, 'eight plus two?'" This is probably the most difficult verbal task. The members of the top group have worked on it considerably longer than those in either of the other groups. The slowest group had had only slight exposure to the operation (although in their language studies they have worked on the reversibility idea using the word *and* and two subjects).

TASK 9: Children were asked to identify the thirteen symbols that have been presented. Eight of the children show complete mastery, and only one could be considered seriously backward in learning symbol identification. Again, the faster groups have been exposed to the full set of symbols for a longer time.

TASK 10: Children were asked to read a relatively simple problem. All children passed on this item.

TASK 11: In this, the easiest of the interpretation tasks, children were asked to solve a problem never presented before: $3 + 5 = a$. To arrive at the solution the child was required to read the problem; then interpret into an operation (a counting operation using fingers); and finally indicate how to change the problem (through substitution) so that it became a true statement. All but one child was able to solve at least one unfamiliar problem.

TASK 12: Children were presented with a standard, simple algebra problem, which they were asked to solve. This is the most advanced level of problem which the children have been presented, and only the top group had worked with it for an appreciable length of time. Four of the five children in this group were able to solve such a problem, and in addition one child in the intermediate group was able to do so.

These results indicate that culturally deprived pre-school children are able to learn formal arithmetic operations when these are presented primarily as part of a language. They are able to read the statements of the language, phrase the open statements (those involving an unknown) as questions, answer the questions, and substitute the answers for the question-asking elements. In short, they are able to learn arithmetic operations from a procedure that places emphasis on the formal meaning, not on the concrete things that are normally treated as primary elements in arithmetic education. Since this procedure enables a more direct, articulate presentation and also ties in with other language skills being mastered by the child, it has great potential application in educating the culturally deprived pre-schooler.

TEACHING READING AS A LOGICAL PROCESS

Among some primary school educators there seems to be a long-standing belief that arithmetic is something intrinsically meaningless to young children whereas reading, if it is taught through suitably lively and realistic materials, is a highly meaningful learning experience. If meaningfulness is defined in any non-trivial sense, however, the exact opposite appears to be true. Arithmetic statements always have counterparts in concrete operations. Arithmetic rules permit of abundant testing in the real world. Moreover, they are marvelously consistent, and a rule that works for some numbers will usually be found to work for all other numbers that the child encounters. Reading, on the other hand, is based on a completely arbitrary and closed set of rules relating printed letters to speech sounds. The rules for decoding print have no applicability to anything outside of reading, and they even run contrary on certain points to cognizing rules that are valid in the outer world (for instance, the rule that a letter may change its identity when it is turned upside-down is directly contrary to the rule governing object identification in the physical world). Moreover, the rules are numerous, unrelated, inconsistent, and incomplete, so that an enormous amount of rote learning is required. There is nothing at all to commend reading instruction except that it is necessary. In teaching arithmetic one can at least take pride in introducing children to one of the more elegant creations of the human intellect; in teaching reading all one can hope for is to make the best of a bad thing.

This pessimistic view could lead one to postpone reading instruction until the child had become sufficiently accomplished in prerequisite skills to learn it in the least possible time and with the least possible effort. Unfortunately, the realities of educational life do not make such postponement practical. In order to progress far in other areas of learning the child must learn to read, and academic progress as a whole is pretty much held down to the rate at which children learn to read. Because culturally deprived children typically have more than their share of difficulty in learning to read, it seems that one should try to give them as rapid a start in it as possible. To delay reading instruction, it seemed, would be merely to dodge one of the major problems in the education of the culturally deprived.

We decided, therefore, to attack the problem of reading head-on, but to try to teach it in such a way as to gain from it whatever secondary educational benefits it might be able to provide. Even though the rules for decoding print are arbitrary and have virtually no transfer value to other problems, they are rules nevertheless, which involve the same logical and language operations as other rules. It therefore seemed that the preferred approach to reading instruction would be one in which children gained a maximum amount of experience in the explicit handling of rules and statements.

Most popular approaches to reading instruction, whether of the whole-word or the phonic type, try to keep rules behind the scenes. In extreme versions of the whole-word approach, reading is taught as if it followed no rules at all. But even in phonic methods, which are worked out on the basis of rules connecting graphemes with phonemes, the rules are not taught explicitly. The child is expected to absorb them unconsciously in the course of practice. These covert approaches to reading may be effective in accomplishing their major objective of enabling children to read, but in keeping the rules hidden they of necessity exaggerate the meaninglessness of the reading process, and deny the child whatever secondary benefits he might draw from working with an at least partly logical system.

By introducing certain artificial restrictions, we were able to reduce the inconsistency and complexity of English orthography and highlight its logical aspects. We restricted the initial vocabulary to three-letter, consonant-vowel-consonant patterns, and avoided use of some of the more troublesome consonants. For further simplification we used only lower case letters. Within this restricted set of words, the following six sets of rules hold:

(1) A word has a beginning and an end. (The beginning is the initial consonant; the end consists of the vowel and the final consonant.) If it has a beginning and an end, it is a word. The beginning always comes before the end.

(2) If the beginnings are the same and the ends are the same, the words are the same and they look the same.

(3) If the words are the same, they sound the same. If the words sound the same, they are the same.

(4) If the words look the same and sound the same, they are the same.

(5) If the endings of the words are the same, the words rhyme. If the words rhyme, the endings are the same.

(6) If the beginnings of the words are the same, the words alliterate. If the words alliterate, the beginnings of the words are the same.

Parts of words were presented to the children on cards, the initial consonant (the beginning) on a white card and the last two letters (the ending) on a yellow card. All letters were printed in black, and the cards contained a black border which served as a cue for orienting and sequencing the cards. Three pieces of three-by-one board were affixed horizontally at different intervals on the back of a standard sized portable chalkboard. The boards were grooved so that the cards could be slid along. The only other addition to this apparatus was an arrow drawn on the middle board which indicated left-right direction.

Rules were taught in the order given above. The following is a sketch of the procedures employed:

RULE 1—a word has a beginning and an end—demanded that we present the words in two parts. This was facilitated by having the beginning and end cards of different colors and lengths. This first rule was a difficult one to teach. To begin with, it was the children's first learning experience in a formal situation. Next we were dealing with culturally deprived children most of whom did not know what beginning or end meant, none of whom had more than about a two-second attention span, and many of whom had difficulty articulating simple words and phrases. We demanded the children's attention by continual questioning; we demanded that they look and respond, with or without understanding. We spent a lot of time trying to improve each child's pronunciation by continual correcting and encouragement. Finally, we got across the idea of beginning and end by always making up each word by a left to right action, taking the white beginning and exaggerating its primacy and directionality and moving it to the center of the display rack and then bringing the end in place with a final motion. Through this latter action we de-emphasized directionality. The second part of this rule—if it has a beginning and an end, it is a word—is a logical extension of the first part. And the third part—the beginning always comes before the end—is a clarification of the first and second parts.

RULE 2—if the beginnings are the same and the ends are the same, the words are the same and they look the same—was important for it taught the children to look for the distinctive characteristics in the elements of each word and to relate the parts as well as the whole to other words. Many of the children had very poor visual discrimination and this rule and the teaching that was necessary to make the rule functional to the children has increased their visual discrimination abilities. This rule has also helped to teach the children the important concept of same and different.

RULE 3—if the words are the same, they sound the same—is an extension of rule 2, and has served to teach the children auditory discrimination as well as more correct pronunciation of the words.

It should be interjected here that in conjunction with the teaching of these rules, we were teaching the phonetic values of consonants which we used with three endings; the total product of which was about fifty words.

RULE 4—if the words look the same and sound the same, they are the same—pulled together everything which we had previously taught them.

RULE 5—if the endings of the words are the same, the words rhyme—was designed to exploit their previous knowledge. The children could now hear different parts of words and to some extent distinguish sounds. By establishing the rhyming rule in their minds, we were setting up the framework for pattern similarities among words. Cat, sat, bat, mat, hat patterning was now not a series of unfamiliar disparate words, but a family of words—all closely related and almost known. After this rule was well learned, we set up endings and began to flip through the initial consonants that they knew. With many of the children rhyming is now a simple process; as the test results show, many of them can use the rhyming principle to figure out unfamiliar words. The children initially showed no ability to recognize rhymes when they heard them. After making little progress in getting them to hear the rhymes in the one-syllable words we were using, we were able to achieve a breakthrough by using a three-syllable rhyming pattern—by using what might be called "overrhyming." A picture of Superman was drawn on the chalkboard and the children were shown how by placing different consonants on his chest one could change his name from *Superman* to *duperman, buperman, guperman, muper-*

man, huperman, etc. The children quickly learned how to determine the name from the letter and to choose the right letter
to go with a name. It was then possible for them to transfer this
to series like *get, net, met, set.*

RULE 6—if the beginnings of the words are the same, the
words alliterate—identified a point of similarity that one finds
over and over again in language. Although teaching the word
"alliterate" to four- and five-year-olds might seem affected, it
really was not, for it identifies for all times a pattern that is often not really recognized until high school poetry classes.
Many of the children benefited right away by being able to
carry on a list of alliterative words to words especially familiar
to them. For example, in one class that has a Tina, a Tony, and
a Steven, Steven finished off this list with a smug look at his
two classmates: *truck, tire, tree, timid, terrible, trouble, time,
table, Tina, Tony.*

After three months of instruction the children have covered
all six rules. How stably they have learned them and how
well they can apply them differs a good deal between children
in the slowest and in the fastest group; however, we have
passed beyond the point where major attention is given to work
with the rules. Compared, for instance, to the number of rules
involved in arithmetic, this is a huge number of rules to master
for children who are so deficient in language structure. We
feel they served the purpose of developing a basic awareness
of what printed words amount to and how they are con-
structed, while at the same time giving them valuable experience in the use of statements; but to hold up progress in reading until the rules were thoroughly mastered would be
unreasonable. They are not, in the end, that essential for learning to read.

Recent work, therefore, has dealt with phonic blending,
figuring out what words are when the ending remains the same
and the beginning changes and vice-versa. Most work has been

concerned with the changing of beginnings—what is popularly called "first-letter phonics."

The over-all progress of the children in reading is quite favorable compared to what we observed previously with culturally privileged children who were younger in chronological age but comparable in mental age but who were taught by a less structured method. The progress is, of course, inferior to what one would expect with children of similar chronological age but with better developed language abilities.

Over and above the children's progress toward learning to read, we are encouraged by the development in the children of a conviction, coupled with some competence, that printed words are things that can be figured out. Had we used one of the more covert approaches to teaching reading, the children might have progressed as far in reading ability, but considering how slow the rate of progress is, it is likely that many of them would have become discouraged and bewildered. As it is, the children have a clear awareness of what they are able to do and why it works. They are solving very difficult problems, problems which might have been avoided by more rote procedures; but by approaching reading as a logical problem they may well be developing abilities and the confidence necessary to deal with logical problems of all sorts. This should in the end pay dividends not only in reading but in all kinds of academic pursuits.

7. A Saturday School for Mothers and Pre-Schoolers

Margaret Lipchik[1]

Although school is imposed on all of us, a small child's dream might be a school where he attends voluntarily one morning a week, where he never experiences failure, and where his mother is not only not far away but may be sitting right in the same classroom with him.

Such an idyllic setup is the experimental Saturday School for Mothers and Pre-Schoolers in Washington, D.C., staffed entirely by Urban Service Corps volunteers. Two nursery school teachers, three elementary school teachers, and a social worker make up the volunteer staff. In addition, an administrator handles registration, and an attractive and friendly mother of ten acts as door knocker, encouraging mothers and their children to attend. The school operates every Saturday during the school year from 10:00 A.M. until noon, interrupted only by a coffee and milk break.

The Saturday School is housed in the Garrison Public School building, located in the heart of the hard-core downtown area of Washington. Many of the children lack basic concepts and attitudes which are important to school success, and the Sat-

[1] Margaret Lipchik, who directed the Saturday School, is Urban Service Corps Assistant in the District of Columbia. Her article appeared in *The National Elementary Principal,* Volume XLIV, Number 2, November 1964. Reprinted by permission of *The National Elementary Principal,* official publication of the Department of Elementary School Principals, National Education Association, Washington, D.C. Copyright © 1964, Department of Elementary School Principals, National Education Association. All rights reserved.

urday School attempts to help ready these four- and five-year-olds for entry into kindergarten and first grade. Their mothers attend with the children and are closely involved in the school activities, learning along with the children.

CREATING A CURRICULUM

Lacking a curriculum, the staff of the Saturday School created their own. Nine categories of desirable skills, habits, and attitudes for four- and five-year-old children were identified. In social relationships, for example, the school tries to help the children learn to work and play co-operatively; to work independently; to share ideas and materials; to be more self-confident; to appreciate and enjoy other children and be willing to take turns; and to gain a feeling of security in a school situation.

Work habits are stressed. The child learns to care for and pick up materials, follow directions, complete a task, and put on and remove his own wraps. Good health and safety habits are developed by teaching the children to use a handkerchief properly; to keep objects out of their mouths; to be neat and clean; and to go to the toilet on their own.

Beginnings are made in literary interests by teaching the children to handle books carefully and respect them. Through storytelling hours, the pupils learn to enjoy stories and begin to look at pictures with more discernment.

On a typical Saturday, the children spend the first fifteen minutes deciding what they want to do and then move toward different interest centers. The teachers plan in advance for many varied activities and use a number of different materials. Block-building, painting at the easel, dramatic play, drawing with large crayons and chalk, looking at books on the library table, working with clay, and many other indoor and outdoor activities are planned for each day and varied from Saturday to Saturday.

Following toileting and snack time, the second segment of

the morning usually consists of group activities which may include singing, experimenting with rhythm instruments, listening to records or a story, and dramatics.

Visual and auditory perception are emphasized and the children are helped to discriminate among sizes and colors. They are encouraged to enjoy music and respond to it and are taught to sing in tune and express their ideas through art media. In the area of language, the children are encouraged to speak clearly in simple sentences; to listen without interrupting; to relate experiences to the group; and to use an adequate vocabulary.

Through trips to the boiler room, the outdoor play area, and the nearby fire station, the pupils gain a simple understanding of their physical environment. Discussions about weather and growing things introduce them to the natural world.

MOTHERS IN SCHOOL

Although many of the children lack desirable concepts and attitudes that should be taught in the home, the Saturday School does not assume that this is the result of parental indifference. Rather, it attempts to build on an interest that is presumed to be present, but not developed.

The mothers are closely involved in the school activities of their children. At the beginning of the school, the mothers were told that in order to make up for the other four days a week when regular nursery schools are in session, they could work with their children at home in a planned attempt to further the concepts, attitudes, and skills which are encouraged in the school. The school program is designed to help the mothers do this. In addition to learning many of the same arts and games that are taught the children, the mothers learn about the early stages of a child's development and discuss aspects of behavior which concern or puzzle them.

While the younger children paint or build with blocks or work with play dough, their mothers observe them in the classroom setting and acquire on-the-spot impressions of their social relationships, work habits, and developing skills. The mothers may also join the circle games, help to mix finger paints, or assume responsibilities in the bathroom or on the playground.

The older children, on the other hand, remain separate from their mothers. On the opposite side of the building, they engage in a program more closely allied to that of a kindergarten. Meanwhile their mothers—who are regarded as "teacher counterparts"—receive parallel lessons, along with an explanation of the values involved for their children.

During another part of the morning, the mothers meet with the staff social worker for talks about problems and challenges in child-rearing and films and lectures dealing with the early stages of child development.

The curriculum for the mothers of the older children developed into a series of "one-shot" activities which paralleled what was offered their children. This group made a trip to the public library where they registered for cards, received a briefing on storytelling techniques, and chose several appropriate books to read to their children at home.

A science lesson alerted them to the opportunity for helping their children to become problem-solvers. The mothers were guided to become good listeners and observers; to be available for trips to the zoo; to provide materials for learning as well as work space in the home; and to explore the house for machines, building materials, and other items that would interest their children. They observed buds and made observation charts for their children to follow as the plants grew in boxes at home.

A lesson devoted to Washington gave parents some background on the city's important buildings and monuments along with an understanding of some of the unique opportunities offered by living in the Nation's Capital. A painting session with a visiting artist proved enjoyably challenging, and a lesson in folk dancing brought fun and laughter.

SOCIAL WORKER ENLIGHTENS, COUNSELS

The role of the Saturday School's social worker has evolved with time. In the beginning, it was important to help the mothers feel relaxed and comfortable. Pertinent movies on child behavior stimulated discussions about many areas of child rearing. At one point, the social worker commented, "Last week we discussed discipline and how it is handled in the homes. This week we moved to the difference in expectations in behavior between home and school, and the restrictions placed upon children by their parents, the extended family, and the Sunday school teacher." Toilet training, babyishness, supervision of play, and how to give instructions were discussed in detail.

A special session was given over to a volunteer woman doctor who discussed medical matters which should concern mothers. At another session, the principal of Garrison School explained school entrance requirements, and the kindergarten teacher talked with the mothers about her expectations for their children. The weekly discussions appear to help, stimulate, and even entertain the mothers.

The social worker observes the children and their mothers in the classroom and talks with the parents about their children's behavior. She has an opportunity to know each parent individually and discuss whatever seems appropriate for that parent and child.

As the social worker has expressed it, she tries "to help the parents know that their children's behavior has meaning, which, when understood, is a key toward unlocking their involvement in learning and making them potentially healthy and happy."

SIZE-UP OF THE SATURDAY SCHOOL

When the Corps conceived the idea of a Saturday School, we were told that we would not get mothers to come to school on Saturday. Yet, despite extremely inclement winter weather during the first five Saturdays, the mothers came in reassuring numbers. They have continued to come, with many benefits to themselves and their children.

After observing the children during their seventh Saturday session, the Garrison School's regular kindergarten teacher commented, "I would say that these children act as my regular kindergarten pupils do by the end of the first report period or nine weeks." In her estimation, our small group taught by two teachers for a total of fourteen hours compared favorably with her kindergarten group of thirty-five children after 135 hours in school.

What makes the crucial difference? The fact that the mothers have taken seriously their home role in the children's school life and make everyday application of the suggestions offered by the staff. Participation by the parents helps bind the home to the school in a pleasant and profitable working relationship.

Whereas both mothers and children were extremely shy and silent in the beginning, they became happily vocal and interested in the offerings of the Saturday School. The children seem to show pride in their mothers' accomplishments, and the unexpected appearance of three fathers indicated the far-reaching influence of the school into the home.

One mother said that her child starts asking on Wednesday, "Is this the day for school?" Another reported that her little boy used to look at television frequently but, since he's been attending school, has become interested in books and in observing plants and flowers. This parent added that she now sees that it takes a mother's help for children to learn. "I've discovered more ways to help my children than I ever knew," said another. "I used to be very impatient with them, but now much of that has changed."

Other mothers report their children to be more relaxed and secure at play than ever before, more helpful around the house, and increasingly independent.

When Saturday School first began, some of the mothers raised their voices to the children, but now they leave the premises more quietly and calmly. They are beginning to reason with their children.

The Saturday School tries to give pre-schoolers emotional security within a group. And mothers who observe and understand the reasons behind their children's behavior in class have irrefutable knowledge of what their children do. This leads them to gain a sympathy for the teacher which develops into a close co-operation with the school.

A promising way of improving understanding of the relationship between school and the home, as well as the larger community, the Saturday School for Mothers and Pre-Schoolers bridges a gap when the parents themselves become part of the program. And early identification of the children's physical and emotional problems can facilitate adjustment to the regular school program when such problems are treated in time.

By showing mothers how to help their children at home, we ought to reduce the number of failures and dropouts and help more children to be successful in school.

Appendix

The following bibliography is probably the most complete working list of useful books and articles presently in existence on pre-school programs and socially disadvantaged children. It was originally published in the IRCD Bulletin, a publication from the Information Retrieval Center on the Disadvantaged, Ferkauf Graduate School of Education, Yeshiva University.

ADAMS, ARLIN M., and CHARLES H. BOEHM, *Proposal to the Ford Foundation for a Pre-School and Primary Education Project.* Submitted for the Council on Human Services of the Commonwealth of Pennsylvania. Harrisburg: Department of Public Instruction, May 1963.

ALMY, MILLIE, "New Views on Intellectual Development in Early Childhood Education." In *Intellectual Development: Another Look.* Washington: Association for Supervision and Curriculum Development, 1964.

ANASTASI, ANNE, and RITA D'ANGELO, "A Comparison of Negro and White Pre-School Children in Language Development and Goodenough Draw-a-Man I.Q.," *Journal of Genetic Psychology,* 81:147–165, 1952.

ANDERSON, H. H., "Domination and Social Integration in the Behavior of Kindergarten Children and Teachers," *Genetic Psychology Monographs,* 21:285–385, No. 3, 1939.

Baltimore City Public Schools Early School Admission Project, *Promising Practices from the Projects for the Culturally Deprived.* Chicago: Research Council of the Great Cities School Improvement Program, April 1964.

BEILIN, H., and L. GOTKIN, "Psychological Issues in the Development of Mathematics Curricula for Socially Disadvantaged

Children." Paper presented to the Invitational Conference on Mathematics Education, Chicago, April 1964.

BERNSTEIN, BASIL, "Language and Social Class," *British Journal of Sociology,* 11:271–276, 1960.

——— "Social Class and Linguistic Development: A Theory of Social Learning." In A. H. Halsey, Jean Floud, and C. Arnold Anderson (eds.), *Education, Economy, and Society.* New York: The Free Press of Glencoe, 1961, pp. 288–314.

BING, E., "Effect of Child-Rearing Practices on Development of Differential Cognitive Abilities," *Child Development,* 34:631–648, 1963.

BLOOM, BENJAMIN S., ALLISON DAVIS, and ROBERT HESS, *Compensatory Education for Cultural Deprivation.* New York: Holt, 1965.

BRODBECK, A. J., and O. C. IRWIN, "The Speech Behavior of Infants without Families," *Child Development,* 17:145–156, 1946.

BRONFENBRENNER, U., "Socialization and Social Class through Time and Space." In E. E. Maccoby, T. M. Newcomb, and E. L. Hartley (eds.), *Readings in Social Psychology.* New York: Holt, 1958, pp. 400–425.

BROWN, F., "An Experimental and Critical Study of the Intelligence of Negro and White Kindergarten Children," *Journal of Genetic Psychology,* 65:161–175, 1944.

BRUNER, J. S., "The Cognitive Consequences of Early Sensory Deprivation." In P. Solomon (ed.), *Sensory Deprivation.* Cambridge: Harvard University Press, 1961, pp. 195–207.

———"The Course of Cognitive Growth," *American Psychologist,* 19:1–15, 1964.

CHILMAN, CATHERINE S., "Child-Rearing and Family Relationship Patterns of the Very Poor," *Welfare in Review,* 3:9–19, January 1965.

CLARK, K. B., and M. K. CLARK, "The Development of Consciousness of Self and the Emergence of Racial Identification in Negro Pre-School Children," *Journal of Social Psychology,* 10:591–599, 1939.

——— "Skin Color as a Factor in Racial Identification of Negro

Pre-School Children," *Journal of Social Psychology,* 11:159, 1940.

DENNIS, W., "Causes of Retardation among Institutional Children in Iran," *Journal of Genetic Psychology,* 96:47–59, 1960.

DEUTSCH, CYNTHIA, "Auditory Discrimination and Learning: Social Factors," *Merrill-Palmer Quarterly of Behavior and Development,* 10:265–276, July 1964.

DEUTSCH, MARTIN, "Nursery Education: The Influence of Social Programming on Early Development," *Journal of Nursery Education,* 19 (3), 1963.

—— "Facilitating Development in the Pre-School Child: Social and Psychological Perspectives," *Merrill-Palmer Quarterly of Behavior and Development,* 10:249–263, July 1964. [Appearing in the present book in slightly revised form.]

—— and ALFRED FREEDMAN, *A Program to Demonstrate the Effectiveness of a "Therapeutic Curriculum" for the Socially Deprived Pre-School Child.* New York: Institute for Developmental Studies, January 1962.

DUNNINGTON, M. J., "Behavioral Differences of Sociometric Status Groups in a Nursery School," *Child Development,* 28:103–111, 1957.

ELKIND, D., "The Development of Quantitative Thinking: A Systematic Replication of Piaget's Studies," *Journal of Genetic Psychology,* 98:37–46, 1961.

FELDMANN, SHIRLEY, "A Pre-School Enrichment Program for Disadvantaged Children," *The New Era,* 45:79–82, 1964. [Appearing in the present book in slightly revised form.]

FOWLER, W., "Cognitive Learning in Infancy and Early Childhood," *Psychological Bulletin,* 59:116–152, 1962.

GRAY, SUSAN W., and RUPERT A. KLAUS, "Early Training for Culturally Deprived Children. Proposed Research Project to Run 9-63 – 8-64," George Peabody College and Murfreesboro, Tennessee, City Schools, 1963.

HESS, R., and V. SHYMIAN, "The Cognitive Environment of Preschool Children." Paper presented to the Research Conference on the Education of the Culturally Deprived, University of Chicago, June 1964.

HILGARD, J., "Learning and Maturation in Pre-School Children," *Journal of Genetic Psychology,* 41:36–56, 1932.

HOFFMAN, M. L., and LOIS HOFFMAN, *Review of Child Development Research,* Vol. 1. New York: Russell Sage Foundation, 1964.

HUNT, J. MCVICKER, "Experience and the Development of Motivation: Some Reinterpretations," *Child Development,* 31:489–504, 1960.

———— "The Psychological Basis for Using Pre-School Enrichment as an Antidote for Cultural Deprivation," *Merrill-Palmer Quarterly of Behavior and Development,* 10: 209–248, July 1964. [Appearing in the present book in slightly revised form.]

JENSEN, A. R., "Learning in the Pre-School Years," *Journal of Nursery Education,* 18 (2):133–138, 1963.

JOHN, VERA P., "The Intellectual Development of Slum Children: Some Preliminary Findings," *American Journal of Orthopsychiatry,* 33:813–822, 1963.

JOHN, VERA P., and LEO S. GOLDSTEIN, "The Social Context of Language Acquisition," *Merrill-Palmer Quarterly of Behavior and Development,* 10:266–275, July 1964.

JOHNSON, NANCY, "Psychological Report Covering Seven Pre-School Centers." New Haven, Connecticut: New Haven Public Schools, June 3, 1964. (Typed manuscript.)

KELLER, SUZANNE, "The Social World of the Urban Slum Child: Some Early Findings," *American Journal of Orthopsychiatry,* 33:813–822, October 1963.

KENDLER, H., and T. KENDLER, "Inferential Behavior in Pre-School Children," *Journal of Experimental Psychology,* 51: 311–314, 1956.

KNOBLOCH, HILDA, and B. PASAMANICK, "Environmental Factors Affecting Human Development before and after Birth," *Pediatrics,* 26:210–218, 1960.

KOCH, M. B., and D. R. MEYER, "A Relationship of Mental Age to Learning-Set Formation in the Pre-School Child," *Journal of Comparative Physiological Psychology,* 52:387–389, 1959.

LARSON, R., and J. L. OLSON, "Method of Identifying Culturally Deprived Kindergarten Children," *Exceptional Children*, 30: 130–134, November 1963.

LURIA, A. R., and S. Y. YUDOVITCH, *Speech and the Development of Mental Processes in Children*. London: Staples Press, 1961.

MCCARTHY, DOROTHEA, *Language Development of the Pre-School Child*. Minneapolis: Institute of Child Welfare Monographs, No. 4, 1930.

MILNER, E., "A Study of the Relationship between Reading Readiness in Grade One School Children and Patterns of Parent-Child Interaction," *Child Development*, 22:95–112, 1951.

MONTAGUE, D. O., "Arithmetic Concepts of Kindergarten Children in Contrasting Socio-Economic Areas," *Elementary School Journal*, 64:393–397, 1964.

MONTESSORI, MARIA, *Spontaneous Activity in Education: The Advanced Montessori Method*. Cambridge, Massachusetts: Bentley, 1964.

MOSKOWITZ, SUE, "Reading in the Kindergarten," *Pathways in Child Guidance*, 7:1–4, March 1965.

The New Nursery School. Greeley: Colorado State College, n.d.

PIAGET, JEAN, *The Origins of Intelligence in Children*. New York: International Universities Press, 1952.

"Pre-Kindergarten: Plenty amid Poverty," *Education U.S.A.*, October 29, 1964.

RAMBUSCH, NANCY M., *Learning How to Learn: An American Approach to Montessori*. Baltimore: Helicon Press, 1962.

SCOTT, J. P., "Critical Periods in Behavioral Development," *Science*, 138:949–955, 1962.

SHEPARD, W. O., "Learning Set in Pre-School Children," *Journal of Comparative Physiological Psychology*, 50:15–17, 1957.

SHIRLEY, M. M., "The First Two Years: A Study of Twenty-five Babies," *Intellectual Development*, Vol. 2. Institute of Child Welfare Monographs Series, No. 7, 1933.

SKEELS, HAROLD M., "An Interim Brief on the NIMH-Iowa Follow-up Studies Relative to Mental Retardation, Dependency and Maternal Deprivation," National Institute of

Mental Health, Bethesda, Maryland, March 31, 1964. (Mimeograph.)

SMILANSKY, S., "Evaluation of Early Education." In UNESCO, *Educational Studies and Documents,* No. 42, 8–17, 1961.

―――― "Progress Report on a Program to Demonstrate Ways of Using a Year of Kindergarten to Promote Cognitive Abilities, Impart Basic Information and Modify Attitudes which are Essential for Scholastic Success of Culturally Deprived Children in Their First Two Years of School." Paper presented to the Research Conference on the Education of the Culturally Deprived, University of Chicago, June 1964. (Israeli Project, unpublished manuscript.)

THOMAS, ALEXANDER, STELLA CHESS, HERBERT G. BIRCH, MARGARET E. HERTZIG, and SAM KORN, *Behavioral Individuality in Early Childhood.* New York: New York University Press, 1964.

THOMAS, D., "Oral Language, Sentence Structure, and Vocabulary of Kindergarten Children Living in Low Socio-Economic Urban Areas." Ph.D. dissertation, Wayne University, 1963.

TOMLINSON, H., "Differences between Pre-School Negro Children and Their Older Siblings on the Stanford Binet Scales," *Journal of Negro Education,* 13:474–479, 1944.

TRAGER, H. S., and M. R. YARROW, *They Learn What They Live.* New York: Harper, 1952.

WANN, K. D., MIRIAM DORN, and ELIZABETH LIDDLE, *Fostering Intellectual Development in Young Children.* New York: Columbia University, Teachers College Bureau of Publications, 1962.

WELLMAN, BETH L., and B. R. CANDLESS, "Factors Associated with Binet I.Q. Changes of Pre-School Children," *Psychological Monographs,* 60, 2 (whole No. 278), 1946.

WORTIS, H., and A. M. FREEDMAN, "The Influence of Environment upon the Development of Premature Children." Paper read to American Orthopsychiatric Association, Chicago, March 1964.

WRIGHT, J. C., and J. KAGAN (eds.), "Basic Cognitive Processes in Children," *Social Research and Child Development Monographs,* 28, No. 2, 1963.